To Marlon,

don't freak out! diff

it represents radically truth is

thoughts — but,

its truth. Talk to me!

Books by Dr. Don Dinkmeyer

CONSULTING:

Facilitating Human Potential and Change Processes (with Jon Carlson)

CONSULTATION:

A Book of Readings (with Jon Carlson)

GENERAL COUNSELING:

Adlerian Counseling (with W. L. Pew, Don Dinkmeyer, Jr.)

GROUP COUNSELING:

Theory and Practice (with James Muro)

SCHOOL COUNSELING:

Theory and Practice (with James Muro)
Counseling in the Elementary and Middle School (with James Muro)

DEVELOPMENTAL COUNSELING AND GUIDANCE:

A Comprehensive School Approach (with Charles E. Caldwell)

GUIDANCE AND COUNSELING IN THE ELEMENTARY SCHOOL:

Readings in Theory and Practice

CHILD DEVELOPMENT:

The Emerging Self

ENCOURAGING CHILDREN TO LEARN:

The Encouragement Process (with Rudolf Dreikurs)

PARENT EDUCATION:

Basics of Adult-Teen Relationships
Systematic Training for Effective Parenting (with Gary D. McKay)

Books by Dr. Gary D. McKay

Systematic Training for Effective Parenting (with Don Dinkmeyer)
The Basics of Encouragement

RAISING A RESPONSIBLE CHILD: *Practical Steps to Successful Family Relationships*

DR. DON DINKMEYER

AND

DR. GARY D. McKAY

A FIRESIDE BOOK
Published by Simon & Schuster Inc.
New York London Toronto Sydney Tokyo Singapore

First Fireside Edition, 1982

Published by Simon & Schuster, Inc.
Simon & Schuster Building
Rockefeller Center
1230 Avenue of the Americas
New York, New York 10020

FIRESIDE and colophon are registered trademarks
of Simon & Schuster, Inc.

Designed by Jack Jaget

Manufactured in the United States of America

10 9
11   Pbk.

Library of Congress Cataloging in Publication Data

Dinkmeyer, Don C.
  Raising a responsible child.

  "A Fireside book."
  Includes index.
  1. Child rearing.   2. Parenting.   I. McKay,
Gary D.   II. Title.
HQ769.D474   1982   649'.1   81-21371
                                           AACR2

ISBN 0-671-21445-4
ISBN 0-671-44749-1 Pbk.

To our wives, E. Jane and Joyce,
and our children,
Don, Jim and Rob

Contents

PART III: THE CHILD AT SCHOOL

PART IV: TOWARD A DEMOCRATIC FAMILY

Chapter 10. *The Family Meeting*

Foreword

The newspapers and television regularly highlight the problems of raising children in today's world. Parents frequently feel defeated and ineffective. Many are bewildered and fearful as they see thrill-seeking, rebellion, and conflict reaching alarming proportions.

Laymen and experts alike expound their theories for our troubles. The "causes" range from broken homes to uncaring parents. Everyone looks for someone to blame.

This book is written in the hope that it will lead to new insights into children's behavior and directions for parent practices that will result in improved communications, more cooperative behavior from the young, and democratic relationships between the generations. The current "generation gap" is only the symptom that points to ineffectual and inadequate relationships existing between many parents and their children.

A child who sees himself as worthwhile and useful has no need to develop destructive patterns. He does not turn to drugs and rebellion. He possesses a cooperative spirit, a sense of responsibility, and positive attitudes toward his family. His relationship with his parents is one of mutual trust and respect.

The family should provide an atmosphere that facilitates such development and nurtures humaneness. Unfortunately, too many families foster conflict and feed the neurotic process.

Generation warfare is only a part of the general rebellion against the Establishment—those in power. The shift from acceptance of autocratic demands made by parents and schools to the demands for one's rights has created today's communication and relationship gap.

Parents have been forced to become involved with an increasing number of complex problems, such as academic underachievement, irresponsibility, apathy, destructive behavior, and drug abuse, to mention but a few. They have been forced to meet these problems with little preparation for the most challenging task in life—being an effective parent. We require licenses for almost all service specialists *but* parents. Parents are expected to do well naturally.

The complexity of parenting has increased because of the shift in our society from autocratic to democratic procedures. But many men still feel superior to women; most adults, superior to children. We are neither trained nor experienced in living with each other as equals. When Father was the boss and all feared to challenge authority, the children may have been unhappy, but there was less conflict. If Father said "Jump," the child needed only to ask "How high?" not "Why?"

Today children are no longer willing to accept a submissive status. Parents have been forced to recognize that the autocratic style can no longer survive. But in retreating from this method of child-raising, too many parents have adopted a permissive approach that fails to regulate or guide, makes no rules, permits chaos, and has inconsistent controls, limits, and motivation.

Currently we witness the results of overindulgence or neglect, both of which show a clear lack of respect for order on the part of both parents and children. We see parents shielding their children from the unpleasant but realistic consequences of life. The child who does not eat regular meals is given special food. He who does not study has his work done for him. Thus the child who is uncooperative and temperamental keeps us at a distance and under his control. Parents can be too demanding, too lenient, or too inconsistent and hence too confusing. The lack of a relationship based upon mutual trust and respect and the failure to understand the basic requirements for effective parent-child relationships result in discouragement. Parents need an understanding of children and guidelines for establishing basic policies.

We are suggesting a democratic relationship that offers choices, encourages participation, planning, and responsibility. It is based on mutual respect and internal motivation. The child functions and cooperates because he has self-esteem and benefits from the values of being responsibly free. He has self-confidence and self-respect and recognizes that he is responsible for himself and hence must either accept the consequences of his behavior or change the behavior. We see discipline as growth from dependence to independence, which is a product of intrinsic motivation.

Parents have been presented with a confusing array of advice through books, magazine articles, newspaper columns, and coffee-klatch conversations with neighbors. The suggestions are not only confusing but often contradictory. Some emphasize the utilization of psychotherapeutic skills. Others simply say "Get tough." The theoretical suggestions and generalizations are many, but the realistic and pragmatic solutions are few.

All of this should make it apparent that raising children is a major challenge. Being a parent has long-lasting consequences for the development of each child and his basic attitudes about self and others. The implications for improving society by increasing effective humanistic communication with the young are great. In order to build courageous, humane, responsible, and communicating new generations parents must change. They must be aware of the importance of their labor of love and devote their thoughts, feelings, and energies to more efficient relationships with their children. In this book when we talk about more efficient relationships we will be suggesting approaches that benefit *both* the parent and the child.

A book is the product of experiences too varied to enumerate. We particularly wish to acknowledge the influence of Rudolf Dreikurs and the staff of the Alfred Adler Institute of Chicago. Their instruction and stimulation provided us with many insights into parent-child relationships.

We believe that there are four basic requirements for producing healthy, mature, and socially responsible children. In brief, these requirements are:

1. Democratic relationships based on mutual respect and a feeling that the child deserves to be treated with both firmness (showing the parents' self-respect) and kindness (showing respect for the child).

2. Encouragement that communicates respect, love, support, and valuing of the child as a person. This can be accomplished verbally or by nonverbal acts showing that the parent cares, as well as by refusing to moralize, compare, or retaliate.

3. The use of natural and logical consequences to replace reward and punishment. This approach enables the child to develop responsibility, self-discipline, and judgment.

4. A basic understanding of human behavior that helps parents to maintain a consistent approach to human relationships.

Before proceeding to enlarge on these four basic concepts we would like to add one last word of advice, a point we will emphasize throughout the book. As parents, you must accept your own imperfections and still have the courage to try to improve. No one can be a perfect parent or raise perfect children. Even if you know all the right things to do, you will not do them all the time. Both you and your children are human. Accept yourself so you can accept your child. Parents who provide growth-promoting relationships will produce children who are unique and autonomous, but who are able to distinguish between anarchy and democracy. They will be neither slaves nor tyrants, but able to use self-interest in a socially responsible manner.

PART I

THE CHILD
IN THE FAMILY

CHAPTER 1

Understanding Behavior and Misbehavior

Parents are frequently puzzled by their child's behavior and seek practical ways to overcome the frustrations misbehavior causes. Although it is interesting and perhaps reassuring to know that Johnny is only "going through a stage," how can his parents survive the child's apathy or rebellion? An intellectual understanding of human behavior is educational but not their primary concern. Parents need a pragmatic method that will improve the behavior of the child and at the same time reduce their own stress.

Upon requesting consultation from the family doctor, Mother is often told, "Don't worry, he'll grow out of it. Most children behave like that at this age." Unfortunately, there is now much evidence indicating that the child who is bad-tempered, nervous, or uncooperative does not necessarily "grow out of the stage." Instead, we are finding that behavior is patterned and predictable and that the child truly is "father of the man."

Frequently the victims of confusing and inadequate information, parents have been told to be more patient by some and more forceful by others. They are advised to be more permissive or simply proficient at mirroring the child's feeling. Most of these suggestions center around the child. But in reality the whole parent as well as the whole child must be consid-

17

ered. For transactions with the child necessarily involve the parents' feelings, attitudes, and values. And as parents we cannot hope to change our children unless we first change our own methods and perceptions. This does not suggest a total personality reorganization, but instead, a development of new procedures and approaches for parent-child relationships. We strive not only to understand our children but to develop better ways to communicate and relate in our effort to build future generations.

Our culture has moved from an autocratic tradition that implied that the parents' word was incontestably correct and final, through permissiveness that set few limits, and now to an attempt to raise children who possess self-discipline and social concern. New democratic procedures, requiring mutual respect, frequently leave parents utterly confused. Their experiences as children in autocratic homes and schools have not equipped them to function democratically. Parents are never sure if they are too strict or too lenient, too demanding or too inconsistent. They only know that what they are doing does not bring about more effective relationships.

Parents have practical questions. They want to know:

"Why is Johnny so annoying? I never seem to be able to give him enough attention."

"Why does Billy always want to be the boss? He tries to control me and get his way. I feel as though I am always the loser!"

"How can I cope with rebellion? What should I do when George is mean and vicious to me and to the rest of the family?"

"Can you help me with Susie? She doesn't participate in school or social life. No matter what I try, nothing works. I have just given up trying to get her involved."

Why is Johnny so annoying?

Mrs. Peterson has four children: Sue, twelve, Ann, ten, Betty, eight, and John, five. She is particularly concerned about John. Unlike the girls, who are cooperative, amuse themselves, and are, as Mrs. Peterson says, "a joy to be with," John is very demanding of her attention and continually in mischief. It is little comfort to think that this is a stage that will pass, since she has had this problem with John for three years. Mrs. Peterson does not need generalities and reassurance—she needs specific help.

Possibly John's position in the family constellation as the youngest and only boy explains his perception of himself as special. However, this does not lead us to corrective action. We must know some specific incidents detailing Mrs. Peterson's and John's behavior.

MRS. PETERSON: I guess the most typical incident would be at suppertime. The girls all help set the table and prepare the food. This is when John chooses to tease them or interfere with their chores.

COUNSELOR: What do you do when this happens?

MRS. PETERSON: I've tried everything, but I'm usually so annoyed that I get after him and tell him what a bad boy he is. Sometimes I spank him.

COUNSELOR: Does this help?

MRS. PETERSON: I guess not, because he's still misbehaving.

COUNSELOR: Do you give John any planned time when you play with him only or do something he likes?

MRS. PETERSON: No, not really. I guess I'm too tired and annoyed after having to fuss with him so much.

COUNSELOR: Does John have any jobs he does for you?

MRS. PETERSON: No, he's really too young to do anything very well.

After more inquiry into the situation, the counselor is ready to make some suggestions:

COUNSELOR: It seems that John feels he is special and must be the center of attention. Perhaps he does this to keep you busy.

MRS. PETERSON: It certainly does keep me on the go.

COUNSELOR: Children become responsible by being given

responsibility. Are there any chores you can have John do
that he would like to do?

MRS. PETERSON: I could have him set the table. He's often
asked to.

COUNSELOR: That's a good idea. I'd also suggest that you
and John pick a time that is strictly John's and do something both you and he will enjoy. If you do something only
the child enjoys, he will recognize your lack of genuine interest. And you yourself will probably dread the activity instead
of anticipating it with the pleasure of a mutually shared experience.

MRS. PETERSON: We could play with one of his games
after supper each night or before bedtime. Is that what you
mean?

COUNSELOR: Yes. Then he will know that he will be spending time with you in the evening and he won't have to pester
you for attention all day.

In this brief vignette we have explored the purpose of behavior and described some concrete suggestions for improving the
relationship between John and his mother. Too often experts
have complicated a problem by giving parents technical explanations, psychological jargon, and clarification of the causes of
behavior instead of supplying corrective actions. Behavior is
best understood when it is recognized that the child always
makes decisions that serve a purpose for him. As one becomes
aware of the child's goal in each interaction, it is possible both
to understand and correct behavior patterns.

CULTURAL MYTHS

Behavior is always influenced to some extent by its cultural
setting. Our children are handicapped by our expectations of
the roles of boys and girls. We anticipate (and anticipation has
considerable influence upon behavior) that girls will conform
and cooperate, while boys will rebel and be lazy. Girls are rewarded for being "Mother's little helper." Boys, on the other

hand, are not given tasks and chores around the house, because these are not considered "manly" responsibilities. Hence girls become tractable and efficient, while their brothers are raised in a *laissez-faire* manner in which rebellion and laziness are accepted as normal. Training the child to fit a stereotype of the "strong man" or the "good woman" hinders the development of his or her full human potential. Instead, the parent can encourage the child to participate and be helpful, recognizing that cooperation is not a sex-related trait.

Another major deterrent to more effective child training is our attitude toward annoying, uncooperative, rebellious behavior. A social conversation among adults about their children reveals that parents regularly tolerate misbehavior as normal, with no expectation that anything can be done.

Mrs. Smith and Mrs. Patterson are discussing their children. Mrs. Smith begins by indicating that Jackie, age ten, is going through an awful stage: "He fights with his brothers constantly, his room is a mess, and his school work is failing. He's just a typical boy."

Mrs. Patterson replies: "Oh yes, I know just what you mean. Billy is about eight, but he's going through the same thing. All children have problems with their brothers and with school."

Let's look carefully at this dialogue. Mrs. Smith describes behavior that is certainly distressing to her, but explains it as a stage. (Follow-up interviews with a counselor usually reveal Jackie's "stage" has been going on for eight years!) In addition, she feels that misbehavior is to be expected from boys. Mrs. Patterson, typically, does not attempt to discuss it further. She, too, accepts lack of respect for order and uncooperativeness as par for the course. She is relieved to hear that her troubled relationship with her son is not unique, and accepts his misbehavior as normal.

We have come to accept misbehavior as normal, and despair of ever changing it. But the problem really lies in our faulty understanding of human behavior and our personal discouragement about ever functioning more effectively with our children. As long as parents remain resigned to being victims, children will continue to be tyrants! Parents—the last unorganized group in terms of their rights—need to recognize that misbehavior is *not* merely a stage or phase. It may be common, but it should not be expected, nor should it be accepted.

Tyranny by children is evidence of an uncooperative, self-centered pattern of life. Like most behavior patterns, it can be modified and dealt with to the benefit of the child, parents, siblings, and the community. Children are not monsters and wild animals by nature. But they do need understanding, guidance, and firm limits to learn to live with others successfully.

Parents who love their children will help them develop their "normal" capacities to be sensitive, caring, socially relating beings. The new culture will expect children to accept their uniqueness, while requiring them to participate in the give-and-take of social living. These children will not only be concerned with doing "their thing" but also with making sure that it contributes to society.

HOW DID HE GET THAT WAY? HEREDITY, ENVIRONMENT, AND THE SELF-CONCEPT

It is not uncommon for parents to attribute their child's misbehavior to a variety of unlikely sources. "Danny is temperamental, and we say he's just like Grandfather." "Becky is stubborn; she got that from her mother." Although it is recognized that children do come into the world with varied and unique temperaments, the probability of direct inheritance of personality traits has not been established.

Heredity establishes the developmental rate of the individual, and determines his basic assets and liabilities. Environmental factors significant to the child's growth include: the family atmosphere, parent-child relationships, the family constellation, relationships between the siblings, and the procedures of child training. Obviously, the factor over which par-

ents can have most control is the method of child training. But
it is also important to recognize the active role that the child
himself plays in his own development. He decides how to use
his potentialities and his environment. He has creative capacity
to place his own meaning on events and to act according to his
own perceptions.

The way in which the child chooses to function provides
insight into his motives and purposes. This self-concept is the
key to understanding his uniqueness. He is not an automaton,
nor does he merely react to external stimuli—he decides. Parents have noticed that at one time being quiet and patient is
effective, while another time it only provokes surliness. The
child has the creative capacity to place his own meaning on the
parents' behavior. If he feels he is being treated unfairly, he
will act on the basis of his perceptions, regardless of the objective facts.

Thus causes are of interest, but they do not determine practical corrective measures. If the child is the youngest, from a
divorced home, or physically handicapped, we can certainly acknowledge these factors. But they should not be used as an
excuse! It is more important to note what the child has decided
to *do* about these situations. All of us can recall children who
function well in such circumstances. Understanding the child's
behavior requires recognition of hereditary and environmental
factors, but correcting that behavior involves working with his
perceptions, attitudes, and values.

BASIC ASSUMPTIONS FOR
UNDERSTANDING BEHAVIOR

Much of the material provided for the parent on child training
has been based on the presentation of general laws and principles. The parent has been told about the average four-year-
old, but has not been given enough information to enable him
to apply it to his own four-year-old, who may be four physi-

cally, six mentally, and three emotionally. While it may be of intellectual interest to understand the average child, it is of greater practical value to comprehend individuality and to become competent at redirecting misbehavior toward actualizing human potential. This *can* be done with effort and does not always require professional assistance.

We believe that each parent will be aided by understanding certain basic tenets related to human behavior. These propositions will enable him to understand behavior and act more effectively in a variety of situations. Parents must learn how to expand their response repertoire with children and how to select responses that are effective.

The child should be understood as a social, decision-making being, whose psychological pattern and style of life have a purpose. The following premises provide general guidelines for specific actions:

1. *Behavior is best understood in terms of its unity or pattern.*

The child always responds as a total being with thoughts, feelings, and actions. Often we deal with the child's actions as if they were isolated when in actuality they are really part of a pattern. The parent must become familiar with the child's beliefs and assumptions about life, for these provide the basis for the child's patterns of behavior, influencing the nature of the relationships the child forms and his willingness to accept responsibility.

Billy's failure to make his bed or clear the table may be related to his unwillingness to keep his desk at school clean or finish his assignments. His habitual failure to respond to order is part of his basic approach to life. He believes it is not necessary for him to cooperate, and he has learned that he eventually wears people down.

As his mother says, "It is easier to do it myself than to make Billy do it." True, it is easier if she is not concerned about helping the child mature. Mothers who perform functions that the child could manage by himself are helping establish a basic pattern of life. Billy has learned that the consequences of his failure to respond to order may be a lecture or scolding, but in the end he gets his way.

The child does not merely react, he interprets situations and decides. His experiences in the family atmosphere, particularly his competition with siblings, are crucial in forming his perception of his experiences. His convictions, attitudes, and values are reflected through his life style as a characteristic pattern of response to life situations.

2. *Behavior is goal-directed and purposive.*

Often parents say, "Johnny's behavior just doesn't make sense. I've done nothing to cause that reaction." Johnny's parents will be able to understand their son's behavior if they approach it in terms of its results. Every psychological action has a goal, and this goal becomes the final cause or final explanation for the act (Adler, 1957). The individual's decision, displayed in his transactions with others, reveals his purpose; thus the consequence becomes the cause for the behavior.

Betty, age five, appears to be bright, but she still needs much help in dressing herself. She is also afraid of the dark and her mother must stay in her room each night until she falls asleep. Let's look at the consequences, and hence the purpose and explanation, of her behavior. By being inadequate, Betty receives special service in dressing and at bedtime. She becomes a princess with a private servant. If her mother does not cooperate, Betty uses emotions—for example, crying—to restore her control of the situation.

Rudolf Dreikurs, an eminent psychiatrist and a leading authority on democratic approaches, has classified the goals of misbehavior as: attention-getting, the struggle for power, the desire to get even or retaliate, and the display of inadequacy or assumed disability in order to escape expectations (Dreikurs, 1968). Betty's demands on her mother manage to gain attention and power, while she maintains a semblance of weakness.

The child who is overly concerned with attention-getting

usually prefers to get it positively, but he will accept negative attention rather than be ignored. Unlike the child who strives for attention by becoming accomplished and industrious, the negative attention-getter is most successful when he is annoying. In both cases the child's behavior requires others to notice and deal with him. He is a specialist at keeping mother and teacher busy with him, no matter whether in praise or reprimand. In order to modify this behavior it is necessary to ignore negative attempts to involve others, while at the same time finding ways to give the child positive attention and recognition, for example, by making special mention of his productive contributions.

The power-seeking individual is out to show that he can control. He refuses to cooperate and will only do exactly what he wants to do. The most common mistake in dealing with this sort of child is to attempt to enforce one's will. This usually only throws coals on the fire and stimulates a greater need for power. Eventual defeat actually stimulates the child to find a more cunning way to control. Parents must learn to avoid this most common reaction because this is the behavior the child is anticipating, and hence their response actually reinforces the misbehavior.

If the child's goal is revenge, he seeks his place by being cruel and disliked. To be called the worst or most horrible is his sought-after trophy. He enjoys mutual antagonism and feels best when others are hurt by him. The parent must recognize that his desire to retaliate contributes to the child's negative self-concept.

The child whose goal is to display disability has developed an approach to life that keeps others from expecting anything of him. He is deeply discouraged, lacks faith in his capacities and powers, and seeks to avoid any anticipation on the part of others that he will be productive and cooperative. The parent must avoid all criticism. He should encourage and recognize any effort, no matter how slight. Focusing on strengths and assets is especially important to this child.

While these goals may seem complex, it is encouraging to know that any parent can learn how to diagnose the purpose of misbehavior by closely observing the psychological transactions and their consequences. He can also check his own spontaneous reaction to the child at the time of misbehavior. This reaction usually points to the child's intentions. If the parent is merely annoyed, the child seeks attention. If the parent feels challenged and wants to control, the child desires power. When the parent is hurt, the child's purpose is revenge. Finally, when the parent despairs and does not know how to get the child to function, it is the child's intention to assume disability in order to escape the parent's expectations.

3. *The way in which the child seeks to be known reveals his self-image.*

Each child, in a unique manner, seeks a place in the family, among his siblings, and in the community. The reputation he tries to establish is derived from his personal perception of success, his self-ideal. We see this in the little boy who, in play, pretends he is a famous athlete. This can also be observed in the child who takes on the role of the cutest, the most helpful, or the most verbal. In some instances the child may develop his reputation via negative traits, such as shyness, stubbornness, or cruelty. Whatever he chooses, he will want to be the best—the greatest athlete, the most helpful girl in the class, or the cruelest boy on the block. Because we live in a culture that emphasizes the value of being superior in contrast to being equal, the child develops a reputation that gives him status, and then he behaves in ways that establish and fortify this image.

The search for significance can motivate the scholar, athlete, singer, ballet dancer, as well as the bully, the brute, and the child who is valued because of his appearance or possessions. To understand and correct behavior patterns, it is vital to perceive the basic master motive or ideal that directs the child's life style. Then the challenge in dealing with his misbehavior is to move it from passive and destructive modes to active and constructive patterns. This is accomplished by emphasizing the child's assets, building his self-esteem and feeling of worth, and eventually redirecting his search for significance toward a more personally acceptable self-ideal.

4. All behavior has social meaning.

The child is a social being, and hence his behavior is best understood when viewed in its social context. When we empathize with the child and see his behavior in terms of his unique social environment, its meaning becomes clear. In most social transactions with peers or parents the child is aware of the consequences and acts accordingly. As we have shown, it is not so bad to be scolded or criticized if you still get your way and get attention besides.

In any given event the child's psychological position and his perception of the meaning of behavior influence his actions. If he is the youngest and believes that everyone is supposed to serve him, then he will behave with that anticipation and expectation. If his experience indicates that generally people permit him special privileges, then these consequences determine the course of his future interactions. He will only change as others fail to fortify his faulty view of life and expect him to function more responsibly.

5. Each child has the creative capacity to make biased interpretations based on his perceptions.

It is basic to recognize that the child gives a subjective, personalized meaning to all transactions. He is regularly interpreting, evaluating, and making decisions about how to react in any given situation.

Sally's mother calls her for dinner, and she does not come. She hears her mother, but does not respond. A second time her mother calls; Sally still does not start to come. Finally Mother screams and threatens, and this time Sally comes. Sally has learned that it is the third call that counts. When she hears the request she determines, by the urgency and the tone of voice, whether this is a last call. From Sally's point of view, coming to dinner only makes sense when she perceives urgency and the possibility of unpleasant repercussions. Her mother's annoyance gives meaning to the event. Mother will learn that calling Sally once and letting her experience the logical consequences of failing to come will be more effective than yelling.

6. *The basic need is to actualize human potential.*

Psychological equilibrium is a product of need satisfaction. Each child has the following psychological needs:

To be loved and accepted.

To be secure and relatively free of threat.

To belong, to identify himself as part of a group.

To be approved and recognized for the way in which he functions.

To move toward independence, responsibility, and decision-making.

As the child's needs are met he attains an inner psychological stability. Failure to feel and perceive self as accepted, loved, secure, approved, and responsible are forces that stimulate misbehavior. The parent can always consider this need checklist when considering reasons for and purposes of misbehavior.

SOCIAL INTEREST

Child training, like any endeavor, requires certain long-range goals. In addition to a concern with developing his child's unique potential, interpersonal experience with the child makes the parent aware of the necessity for encouraging social interest or the child's capacity to give and take. The child with social interest is cooperative and respects the rights of others. He has a sense of his worth and a feeling of belonging. He is courageous in the pursuit of goals that reflect not only self-interest but social concern. Our goal as parents is to raise children who will be psychologically mature individuals, capable of adjustment, and, more important, able to contribute in a socially responsible manner.

FAMILY INFLUENCES ON THE STYLE
OF LIFE

Family atmosphere

The child first learns to be human in the social unit of the family. The family provides the environment and the setting that expose the child to a set of assumptions about life. The commonly held traits, beliefs, and values arise from this atmosphere, as do the various means of relating to others. The child observes family relationships and exchanges and interprets these as the way to deal with other people. If his mother and father quarrel, or if one of them uses temper or feelings to gain control, the child observes closely and then adopts the procedures that appear to be effective.

Families that emphasize working together for mutual interest often stimulate this attitude in the child. If the family as a whole values intellectual pursuits, music, or athletics, often the children pursue these interests.

The family pattern is not to be understood as a direct determinant of behavior. Obviously the child is free to accept or reject the pattern. However, when siblings have similar character traits, it is frequently an expression of the family atmosphere which has been internalized. Differences in the personalities of siblings is a result of position and competition in the family constellation and of the individual's perceptions.

Family constellation

Each child has a distinct position in the family. This position influences his perception of life. The ordinal position (actual numerical position as oldest, second, middle, youngest, or only child) frequently results in certain characteristic attitudes and traits.

The classical descriptions of ordinal positions usually suggest:

The oldest child is for some period an only child, who is eventually dethroned. He is concerned about continuing to be first, and when he cannot be first, he may give up. If he cannot be the best in a useful way, he may decide to be the worst, which is another way of being first.

The second child may originally feel inferior to the older child. He then will compete and attempt to overtake his sibling. He often appears to be working hard to catch up. If there is considerable competition between the two, the second child will usually become more of what the first is not, while giving up in areas where he does not believe he can succeed. He may come to surpass the sibling in academics, athletics, or sociability, for example.

The middle child may feel squeezed out of the rights and privileges of the other children. He will either give up and feel that life is unfair or he will succeed in overcoming both competitors.

The youngest child is the baby, and he can turn this to his advantage. More often than not he establishes a special place for himself, frequently through characteristics that are passive and nonproductive. He may become the cutest, the most charming, or the most helpless.

Because the only child spends his developmental years in the company of adults, he develops traits that win him the attention and assistance of adults. Thus he may feel that he is a member of the adult elite and entitled to his own way.

Birth order is never considered to be a determinant. The child has the creative capacity to choose his role in the siblingship. His place in the family constellation provides clues, but we must always determine how the child has perceived and used his place (Dreikurs and Soltz, 1964).

METHODS OF TRAINING

The child is also significantly influenced by the methods of training employed by his parents. If the methods feature faulty approaches, such as spoiling, nagging, or excessive supervision, the child will not be allowed to experience consequences and will not be able to learn from the order of life. Protecting the child from the logical consequences of his decisions and actions by substituting nagging and punishment destroys the parent-child relationship and prevents the child from becoming independent and responsible.

The following principles should undergird the parents' approach to child management:

1. The parent should understand the child and the purpose of his misbehavior.

2. The relationship between parent and child should always be one of mutual respect.

3. Parents should be both firm and kind—the firmness indicating respect for themselves, and the kindness showing respect for the child.

4. The child should be valued as he is. His assets and strengths should be discovered, valued, and emphasized. A parent should spend more time encouraging than correcting him. One positive statement a day is a good motto.

5. Parents should have the courage to live with their own inadequacies. They should accept themselves as well as their child.

6. Parents must act more and talk less. Natural and logical consequences that teach a respect for order should replace reward and punishment.

7. If a poor or ineffectual relationship exists, parents must have the patience and take the time to make corrective efforts. Developing human relationships that are mutually satisfying requires awareness, but is worth the effort.

The parents play a major role in the formation of the child's life style and personality. Their dialogue often directly affects the child's self-concept. Phrases that are negative and nagging, that point out faults, tend to build feelings of inadequacy or resistance. Words that focus on assets, that are positive and encouraging, tend to build self-respect and self-esteem. The parents' real success and joy come from seeing the child emerge as an autonomous and independent individual who is at the same time secure enough to be responsibly interdependent with his parents and society. No job well done is ever easy. Being a parent must be "worked at," and rewards will follow.

REFERENCES

Adler, Alfred. *Understanding Human Nature.* New York: Premier Books, 1957.

Dreikurs, Rudolf. *Psychology in the Classroom* (2nd ed.). New York: Harper & Row, 1968.

———— and Vicki Soltz. *Children: The Challenge.* New York: Duell, Sloan & Pearce, 1964.

CHAPTER 2

Understanding and Promoting Emotional Growth

Emotions involve the feeling life of the individual. Billy gets a new toy, and he is happy. Bobby takes the toy away, and Billy is angry. They fight over the toy and break it, and Billy is sad. Billy goes to his mother seeking sympathy, and he may find her angry with him for destroying the toy. Emotions are an important part of every transaction between parent and child. However, because parents are often poor listeners, they do not even hear the feeling. In other instances they choose to ignore the feeling and even encourage the child to forget the feeling. In this manner we deny the child the growth of his total being. For without awareness of his feelings he cannot be in touch with himself, nor can he become sensitive to others.

Emotions may be positive forces that serve to energize and enrich an experience. They can be a source of strength and motivation. Or emotions can disorient, disrupt, and create social alienation. Many believe that almost all learning is acquired in emotional terms. Emotions give life its color, richness, and completeness by being a part of all our experiences. We "love" to play a sport, or we "hate" to practice our music. Our emotions have a powerful influence on our behavior and attitudes and affect our perception of a situation.

In some instances emotions bring us together with people, as in the cases of joy and sympathy; while the contrasting feelings of anger and sadness may cause a separation. Since each child will experience the full range of pleasant and unpleasant feelings, the parent should help him understand and become comfortable with his feelings.

PURPOSIVE EMOTIONS

Emotions are sometimes viewed as mystical forces totally beyond control. We say, "I'm so angry I can't think" or "I was so afraid I forgot." It is important that parents understand and recognize that emotions can also be purposive, helping a child to attain a goal. Emotions generally support the intentions of the individual and are often used to modify a situation to one's advantage.

The grandparents are visiting, and during a shopping trip Billy, age four, wants a car in the toy section of the store. His mother indicates that he already has many cars like it and they cannot buy another one. Billy starts to pout and cry. The grandparents are sympathetic. They intercede and say they will buy the car for Billy. Billy has learned that emotions in the form of water power serve a purpose—they help him get his way.

It is time for Joan, five, to go to bed, but she complains that she is not ready. Getting no response except a firm "Get going now," she resorts to crying. Father, moved by her tears, agrees to accompany Joan to her room and read her a story. She becomes special, and earns attention and service through the use of emotions.

During incidents with emotional overtones the parent should ask himself, "What does my child accomplish by being so emotional? What does he expect me to do?" Awareness of the social context in which the emotion occurs helps the parent to understand the goal-directed nature of emotions, and he becomes aware of the way in which the child chooses a certain emotion to provoke a certain response.

Feelings are always present, and the parent must become more skillful in recognizing their potential value. Even if they are negative, it is not productive or healthy to teach the child to deny his feeings. Emotions are capable of generating genuine involvement as well as forcing others to cooperate or give in to our demands.

GOALS EMOTIONS MAY ACHIEVE

Parents can recognize how emotions can serve purposes and intentions by noting characteristic situations in which purposive emotions may be employed:

1. Emotions may be used to get special attention. When a child is especially sad or temperamental, he may receive special treatment and sympathy. The emotion enables him to get the extra service and attention he would not obtain in another way.

Jimmy has lost his football and the game has to stop. The boys decide to go to another field where Sam has a ball. Since Jimmy doesn't own the new ball, he can't make the rules or conditions for play. But Jimmy is accustomed to making the rules, and now he is not willing to go along with the rules Sam has made. At home Jimmy complains about the other children. His parents console him, and although Father is very busy, he feels compelled to make a special trip to replace the football. Because Jimmy is treated special at home, he continues to try to get similar treatment from the other boys.

2. Emotions may be used to control. The temper tantrum and displays of anger often bring power to the child and enable him to control the situation.

The teacher changes Jack's seat at school. He is moved from the front of the room, and therefore he is no longer the errand boy, nor does he get special attention. He becomes very angry, pouts and fusses until the teacher finally gives in and returns him to his former place.

3. Emotions can serve the purpose of retaliation for what is thought to be unfair treatment.

The boys are deciding on a game to play. Fred wants to play basketball, but the other boys choose baseball. Fred does not get his way. He becomes angry and starts to fight with John, who had persuaded the boys to play baseball. He feels it is fair to fight since John was against him.

4. Emotions can be used to protect us from functioning. When we are discouraged we may use sorrow or weakness to get support and special service.

Sally gets very "nervous" whenever she is asked to stand and spell a word. She becomes confused, incoherent, and whimpers. The teacher feels sorry for Sally and indicates that she does not have to spell orally. Sally has learned how to control through emotions.

Emotions are of positive value when they elicit our concern or empathy for the feelings of others. This increased sensitivity improves social relationships. Even temper may have a value insofar as it is a way of helping the child stand up for his rights when he is defeated or frustrated. However, when temper (usually in the form of tantrums and demands) is used to control others, this self-centeredness impedes full emotional development.

How can the parent correct negative use of emotion? The temper tantrum is an interesting example of this kind of behavior. When the child is temperamental, the natural tendency is to show him that he can't get away with it. We become emotionally involved, trying to prove that we cannot be manipulated this way. Depending upon the situation, the parent may attempt to outshout the child, scream at him, or try to control. If others are present and the parent is embarrassed, he may attempt to bribe his child to stop the temper display. These reactions only maintain or intensify the tantrum. The child's sense of timing in regard to control is usually far superior to the parent's natural ability to help him grow emotionally. However, the parent must learn to help the child understand and manage his feelings.

Since the temper tantrum is usually an emotional show, it requires an audience. The most effective procedure in dealing with a temper tantrum is to leave the child alone. When dealing with a temper tantrum it is most important not to be intimidated because of the presence of friends, relatives, or strangers.

FEAR AND ANXIETY

It is normal to anticipate that the young child may be fearful at times. He may be afraid of loud and unexpected noises or of strangers. These types of fears can be valuable for the survival of the child. But fear and anxiety are often a product of personal perceptions in combination with creative imagination. One must distinguish between fears that may be reality-based and those that are the product of biased perceptions or are created by the child for a specific purpose.

Children appear to be born relatively free from fear. But an adult's overanxious or oversolicitous behavior can cause fear to arise. If his parent is fearful and not sure that the child will succeed, the child will almost always live up to this expectation. Often the child operates with an awareness of the social consequences of his behavior. For example, his fearfulness may win him special service or control over others. While there are situations that merit caution and an awareness of dangers, protecting the child from certain harmless and valuable experiences only inhibits his emotional growth.

The child should develop courageous but reasonable approaches within the limitations involved in walking in traffic, using potentially hazardous tools, or playing with animals. There are a number of training procedures that can be used to teach a cautious approach to real danger. They involve the stimulation of the child's intelligence, enabling him to distinguish between what is a valid opportunity or gamble and what is a foolish risk or chance.

When a child is fearful he should have access to someone who is willing to listen and understand. Often the opportunity to ventilate in the presence of an empathic person is effective in coping with the fear. After the child has expressed his apprehensions, the parent can reflect his understanding of what he is experiencing. Once the child is aware of parental support, the parent and child together can explore ways to overcome the fear.

> TIM: I don't want to go into the pool.
> PARENT: It seems very dangerous to you.
> TIM: I might sink.
> PARENT: Since so many of your friends swim, would you like to play in the water too?
> TIM: I'm not sure I could.
> PARENT: Let me help you by the side of the pool.

This approach is characterized by understanding and accepting the fear first and then helping the child to lose his fear. Never laugh at fear; to the child it is very real and threatening.

In other instances fear may purposefully be used to control adults. The parent should avoid preaching, blaming, manipulating, bribing, cajoling, and begging. He should not become involved in excessive talking. If the parent is unimpressed by fears but supportive of the child, the purpose for being fearful is eliminated.

> Mr. and Mrs. Z.'s six-year-old daughter Brenda was afraid of sleeping by herself in her room. Both parents had repeatedly reassured her that there was nothing to be afraid of. Despite their efforts, Brenda continued to be afraid. She cried, screamed, and often fled to her parents' bedroom for comfort. On many other nights her mother would have to go to Brenda's room and stay until she fell asleep.
>
> One night Mr. and Mrs. Z. decided to try a different approach. They told Brenda that they felt she was a big girl and

capable of sleeping by herself. They informed her that the door to their bedroom would be locked and that they would not come to the door or go to her room.

Later that evening they heard Brenda whining. Although Mrs. Z. was tempted to go to the door, she refrained from doing so. In a few minutes Brenda began screaming and pounding on the door, complaining that she was afraid and pleading with her mother to please accompany her to her room. Mother made no response. After several minutes of screaming Brenda began to quiet down and eventually became silent.

In the morning Mr. and Mrs. Z. found Brenda sleeping on the floor outside their door.

The next night Brenda tried again to get her mother to pay attention to her fears. Again she was unsuccessful. After that, Brenda stopped trying to get her mother to come into her room.

The fear of rejection is one of the special fears children often need help with. Often a child gets most of his status from belonging and being accepted. When his position is dependent upon approval, he may be afraid of making a mistake. This type of fearful approach is best corrected by helping the child see that his parents accept him as he is.

Susie was an outstanding fourth-grade student and received much praise for her schoolwork. The class was now beginning some new arithmetical processes which she was not able to master immediately. Her mother noticed that instead of the usual eager presentation of her arithmetic papers, there appeared to be no arithmetic papers at all. While cleaning Susie's room she found a paper with many mistakes and a note from the arithmetic teacher: "This work is not up to your standards." Susie's exaggeration of the danger of mistakes and her fear that she was no longer acceptable to her parents had led her to hide the paper.

The next afternoon Susie's mother asked how things were going in arithmetic. Susie began to cry and told how difficult it had become. Her mother's acceptance of her feelings and her assurance that she understood enabled Susie to bring out the papers, seek assistance, and begin to realize that she could learn from her mistakes.

The fear of the dark may be genuine or purposive. The parent must accept the fear and listen to and understand the reason behind it. Experiences in which the child gradually controls the dark through the use of lights help him learn to control this fear.

> Joe, age five, was afraid of the dark and insisted that one of his parents stay in his room with him until he fell asleep. As soon as they started to slip out after a time he called and fussed. This served to keep the parents captive.
>
> JOE: Don't go. It's too dark.
> MOTHER: When there is no light, you are frightened.
> JOE: It's very scary.
> MOTHER: I am going to put a lamp in your room. That way you can turn it out yourself when you are sleepy, or I'll turn it off when I go to bed.

The fear of school is frequently related to a fear of separation from parents. It is also a way of controlling the parents by eliciting sympathy.

> Bonnie refused to attend school. Whenever it was time to go she would dawdle, have a temper tantrum, or pretend she was ill. These methods usually immobilized her parents. Either they became involved in a power struggle or they gave up. After seeking professional advice they tried a new approach. They indicated to Bonnie an understanding of her feeling, encouraged her to express her fear, and explored ways to deal with it—but they firmly insisted she go to school.
>
> MOTHER: It's time for school.
> BONNIE: I can't go. I'm sick.
> MOTHER: You don't feel well?
> BONNIE: My stomach hurts and I feel very weak.
> MOTHER: You are afraid something might happen at school.

BONNIE: I don't like the kids, and the teacher is mean to me. They are *all* very mean. I hate them and school. I won't go.

MOTHER: I know you are very angry and scared, but you *are* going to go with me.

BONNIE: I won't!

Mother securely grasps Bonnie's hand and leads her to the car. While it is important to listen to her feelings, it is equally important to provide a firm but kind resolve that Bonnie is going to school.

Fear of school often indicates a lack of independence. Does the child get special attention, a sense of winning, or receive pity? Does the child cause his parents discomfort? The fear is often complicated by parents who feel inadequate because they should be able to get their child to go to school but cannot. The accompanying social embarrassment the parents experience tends to reinforce the behavior. Professional consultation may be necessary if the situation persists.

PROMOTING EMOTIONAL GROWTH

Emotional maturity is always relative. A child may be very mature in his feelings about work and responsibilities and at the same time he may be quite immature in terms of his relationships with other children. Emotional maturity fluctuates because emotional development is not steady and continuous. And, similarly, emotional flexibility and capacity to cope may vary from day to day and from situation to situation. The child becomes able to conquer a fear in one area while acquiring anxious feelings in another. For example, he may be able to accept defeat in games while becoming despondent about a single mistake on a school paper.

Adults as well as children are continually working toward the integration of beliefs, feelings, attitudes, and actions. As we are permitted to be open, honest, and free to relate our feelings, we become more sensitive to self and others. We cannot expect emotional growth to proceed like physical growth, for it experiences reverses. But as parents permit the child to become independent and self-sufficient, he begins to accept responsibility for his behavior, and emotional maturity is facilitated and promoted.

CONDITIONS FOR EMOTIONAL GROWTH

Emotional growth proceeds best under the following conditions:

1. *In a democratic climate whose equalitarian premise is concerned with equal rights and responsibilities.* The democratic atmosphere provides freedom that is naturally accompanied by responsibility. The child learns from the social and natural order that although he is free to play with his friends, do his work, or tease an older brother, he must be prepared to accept the responsibilities and consequences that follow from his choice.

2. *When the climate encourages open expression of feelings, whether negative or positive.* It is not only permissible but expected that one express his real feelings. When parents try to change feelings by denial and repression they encourage holding emotions in, and this eventually produces depression, anger, and rebellion.

Because the parent has lived longer does not entitle him to ignore what the child is saying and feeling. Even more important than understanding the content of the child's message is recognizing the feelings that underlie it. The parent must listen for the emotions that the child expresses, and he must respond empathetically, for empathy is essential to stimulate emotional growth.

As the parent becomes more attuned to the child's language and becomes a more experienced listener, he can help the child become aware of the intentions, purposes, and goals behind his emotions. Then, as the child becomes self-aware, the parent can begin to discuss with him better ways to reach his goals by participating in the give and take of life.

3. *When the child is ready for a new experience.* This readiness should include physical, social, and motivational factors. Parents may push the child into physical or mental activities in which *they* have ambitions for him, although the child may not yet have the coordination, social confidence, or interest to provide the necessary foundation for success.

4. *When the parent ignores negative behavior—thus often eliminating it.* It is easy to be "hooked" by bad behavior. The parent must guard against reinforcing, encouraging, or attending to misbehavior. However, at the same time the parent must look for positive elements in the behavior or attitudes which can be encouraged. Rather than focusing on Billy's poor choice of friends, parents should emphasize how pleased they are to see that he is getting to know more people.

5. *When the parent-child relationship is neither overprotective nor oversolicitous.* It must involve mutual respect and an atmosphere in which the child is encouraged to join in new experiences and is allowed to learn from them.

Billy comes home enthusiastic about joining the Little League, and his mother immediately thinks of the additional demands on herself for driving, supervision, and attendance at games. She is also aware of the pressures involved in competitive baseball. But despite her hesitations, this is a time for Billy's mother to avoid being overprotective and encourage her son to get involved in a new learning experience.

6. *For the very young child who shows interest in a new skill or hobby, if his parents can make resources available which will insure some success.* Encouraging positive efforts and avoiding comparing him to more experienced children will allow the child to take small but positive steps. He will learn the joy that comes from participating in self-selected experiences.

COMPETITION

The capacity to be competitive has value when it enables an individual to move toward self-initiated goals inspired by social interest and concern for society. Self-competition that helps the individual play music more beautifully or improve his skills to become a better member of a team are examples of self-competition and social interest. However, while we want children to excel, we must be careful not to misuse competition.

The ineffectual competitor is frequently a child whose parents set standards that are too high or blame him for failures. In these cases the child loses his self-confidence altogether or harbors the false belief that his real worth depends upon his being first or a winner. He believes that any loss or failure will diminish his self-esteem and value. Consequently he retreats from all competition, thinking that it is better not to try at all than to try and possibly fail. The youngest child in a family of exceptional athletes may decide not to play sports because he believes he cannot live up to the standards of his predecessors.

Competition and bribery should never be used to motivate. The child who is intensively competitive feels his job is never completed; overambition is often the product. For the child always strives for more than he can possibly achieve, and his distorted standards leave him continually dissatisfied and discouraged. Constant failure is a sign of overambition. Parents can help the child understand and accept occasional failure as a fact of life by publicly acknowledging their own mistakes without complaining or moralizing.

Parents often expect their child to compete in areas of their own ambitions. The child may perceive that the parents expect outstanding results in school or athletics, for example. If he believes he can't meet the expectations of his parents, he may either compensate in other areas or offer his inadequacy as an excuse for not competing. Parents must de-emphasize exaggerated personal goals of achievement.

Value what the child is doing instead of evaluating it. We do not grade and hold our friends to standards. If we did, we would lose them! The child benefits more from being valued than evaluated. While the parent may accept his feelings of uncertainty and fear of failure as realistic, he must assure the child of his worth and acceptance regardless of his achievements. The child should come to feel that a good effort alone makes him worth while. Parents must be more concerned with attitudes and the courage to try than with meeting high expectations. The courageous child learns to set goals that are realistic. His maturity involves developing standards that are internalized and personally satisfying.

DEALING WITH DISCOURAGEMENT

The child who feels inadequate or defeated manifests discouragement. He does not believe he can satisfy himself or others. A discouraged child may use his emotions to avoid facing the tasks of life.

When dealing with the discouraged child it is important to de-emphasize external standards. Let him know that he is performing well, and accept his attempts and efforts. Let him know mistakes are to help us learn.

> Susie was painting a picture. She hesitatingly looked at the range of colors and then asked her mother for a suggestion. Mother declined to comment and only smiled.
>
> SUSIE: Should I take the yellow or orange?
>
> MOTHER: You don't know which color to choose?
>
> SUSIE: What will be the best?
>
> MOTHER: It's your picture and whatever you like will be fine.
>
> SUSIE: What do you want?
>
> MOTHER: I know you would like me to choose for you, but I like your ideas.
>
> SUSIE (pointing to yellow): Will yellow be okay?
>
> MOTHER: Whatever *you* decide will be fine.

CHAPTER 3

Mistaken Concepts of Adults and Children

THE FALLACY OF THE "GOOD" MOTHER

Why I stopped being a "good" mother—a "reformed" mother's testimony.

There are certain things a "good" mother always does. Let's see if you do any of them. Do you help your child get dressed? Do you call him to dinner more than once? Do you tell him to have a good day at school while sending him hidden messages: "Behave yourself," "Do what I want you to," "Make me proud of you"? Do you ask him if he had a good day (another way of checking to see if he fulfilled your ambitions)? Do you lay out his clothes? Do you tell him when to go to bed and when to get up? When to put on his pajamas? When to go out to play? When to watch TV? How much food to eat or not to eat? When to clean up his room or to help around the house? When to do his homework?

Do you understand that all the preceding communications and hidden messages are practiced by parents who have good intentions but faulty methods?

In short, "good" mothers of this vintage do a lot of talking, get little results, big headaches, and often do not enjoy their children. A "good" mother doesn't give the child a chance to grow to be responsible because she is too busy being the responsible one. Children, as equal human beings, deserve the right to make choices and decisions for themselves. How can

47

mothers learn to be quiet and let the children grow? By doing just that—stop talking! When she is successful the child will tune her "in" instead of "out"! *

The role of Mother in our society is often misunderstood. A mother may feel that in order to be "good" she must dominate family affairs and be able to control her children. She may feel personally responsible for everything they do, and act as if their misbehavior is a reflection on her capabilities as a mother.

A "good" mother believes that everything she does is for the sake of her children. However, if her motives were truly altruistic she would be less concerned about her image as a mother and more devoted to promoting feelings of adequacy in her children. She would try to stimulate a sense of cooperation and responsibility arising from within each child rather than applying external pressures that only prove her own self-worth. Billy learns responsibility better by being given the chance to choose a job that will contribute to the family than if he is assigned a task. The child's interest, the freedom of choosing, and his feeling of satisfaction with a job well done will help him attain the long-range goal of responsible adulthood and will make Mother's job of guiding him that much easier.

All of us have known families where all the children have developed a high degree of social interest. Their parents appeared to be naturals at the task of parenthood. Unfortunately, there are very few "naturals." Most mothers feel insecure in their position. This is due to a society that is expert in discouraging its members. We are so mistake-oriented that it is extremely difficult to learn from our mistakes in child training. The mother whose child is not succeeding by the standards of the culture often considers this to be a reflection on her ability. Poor report cards, few friends, shyness, ineptness in athletics

---

* Excerpt from a revised mimeographed handout, "I Stopped Being a 'Good' Mother," originally developed by Doloris Chestnut, former member of the Parent Study Group Program sponsored by Adult Education in Parkway School District, St. Louis County, Missouri.

should not be viewed as parental failure any more than success in these areas indicates accomplished parenting.

Many mothers feel it is their job to protect their children. Of course there are some situations in which a child is physically incapable of dealing with problems and needs protection. But areas of a child's life with which he cannot cope are far fewer than most mothers believe. A mother who overprotects views her child as incapable of dealing with life. Her behavior reflects her own insecurity. She proves her worth by keeping the child dependent on her.

> BILLY: I can't tie this shoe.
> MOTHER: Come here, I'll do it for you.
>
> JOHN: How do you cook the hot dogs, Mother?
> MOTHER: Never mind, the stove is dangerous, I'll do it.

This type of protection keeps the child from growing up and maintains the illusion of Mother's great importance. She becomes the martyr, often relating how much she has to do—"See how I suffer." The real pity is that both mother and child lose in "smother love."

Although we have referred to the concept of the "good" mother, we must emphasize that " 'good' motherism" is not necessarily restricted by the sex of the parent. The concept refers only to an attitude. In other words, some fathers are also "good mothers." In most cases, however, mothers are the greater victims to this concept than fathers because of the cultural expectations of a woman's role.

The effects of these misconceptions on the child

The "good" mother affects each child in a unique way.

In most families of more than one child at least one of the children stands out as more cooperative than the others. He is generally successful in approximating Mother's standards, and when he does step out of line he is easily redirected. Most parents do not recognize the discouragement that prevails in this "good" child's life. He often feels he must be good in order to secure a place in the family. His efforts are directed toward impressing others and himself with his "goodness." He behaves cooperatively not solely to make life more pleasant but rather for the purpose of superiority—"Look how good I am!"

But the "good" child does not necessarily surpass his siblings in all areas. For example, he may feel he cannot shine academically and yet be the most congenial and cooperative at home, or conversely, he may be an excellent student and completely irresponsible at home. In an effort to maintain his superiority the "good" child avoids situations where he feels he cannot prove his "goodness."

The discouragement of the "good" child becomes quite evident when another child begins to improve in the areas in which he maintains superiority. The "good" child often begins to slip—he may even become the "problem" child. This phenomenon of role reversal happens often, and it shocks and discourages parents. What they do not realize, however, is that this role reversal is actually a sign of progress, for now they have the opportunity to help the "good" child develop new relationships based on real cooperation and social interest rather than on superiority. By refusing to make comparisons and by encouraging any attempts to be mutually supportive, parents now can reduce the competition and strengthen the cooperative spirit between the children.

A child who feels he cannot secure a place through contributions and cooperation switches to the mischievous side of life to find a niche. The misbehaving child is very successful in gaining recognition from his parents. Although he would probably prefer positive recognition, he chooses negative attention rather than be ignored—"If I can't gain my parents' approval, I can at least be important by making trouble."

Some children choose the role of the clown. The clown jokes continually and makes few contributions. He masks his feelings of inadequacy by making everything funny, keeping his mother upset and busy with him. At school the clown entertains his peers and at the same time annoys and frustrates his teacher by interfering with her attempts to teach. The reactions of his audiences provide him with the recognition he desires.

Many children respond to Mother's behavior by choosing the role of the boss. The boss attempts to force others to give in to him. He strives to get his own way, often gets it, and only feels adequate when he is in control. He defeats Mother's efforts to get him to do anything he doesn't want to do. If she succeeds in forcing him, he does not perform to her satisfaction. He may try to retaliate for having to do what he does not want to do. In the classroom he defeats the teacher. He may refuse to study and learn, keep the classroom in turmoil, or bully his peers. His strivings for power are met with resistance, pressure, or acquiescence. And these reactions increase his desire for power.

Almost all children react to "good" mothers' standards and methods with some degree of discouragement. Since they cannot live up to Mother's standards, they lose confidence in themselves and begin to feel inadequate. They become irresponsible, since Mother is busy being the responsible one. And they become defeated, since they find that they can do little that is good enough. Children may succumb to these feelings by resisting efforts to force their cooperation, or by giving up, passively accepting whatever is done to them in the hope that they will be excused.

"Good" mothers are frequently victims of feelings of inadequacy too, since they experience little success in influencing their children. They feel unappreciated, ineffective, and not respected. Both mother and children become expert at discouraging each other, and accept their difficulties as inevitable.

THE PARENTS' REAL ROLE

Parents carry with them a lot of assumptions they have learned in growing up which they treat as realities, such as: it is right to keep up a pretense that all is well when it isn't, work is good, and acquiring things is important. The assumptions were often useful to them during their own childhoods; however, the rapid rate of social change does not make these assumptions realities for this generation. It is obvious that hair styles, fashions in dress, and music preferences are but a few of the areas where old assumptions are no longer valid. These are areas in which parents must learn to listen and engage in meaningful dialogue with their children.

1. *Provide a healthy atmosphere*

Too often the atmosphere of the home is charged with hostility between parents and children. Autocratic methods that fail stimulate frustration, defeat, and ill feelings toward the child. The child resents the parent's efforts to control and deny him his rights, and cooperation is misunderstood as giving in to parental demands. If the parent trains the child to be highly competitive, then cooperation may even be considered a sign of weakness. Both parent and child feel trapped in their dilemma.

To provide a healthy atmosphere, which facilitates growth and cooperation, the parent must learn to accept and respect his child, to treat him as an equal person entitled to basic human rights. The parent must learn to listen to and encourage his child, to promote a sense of responsibility, and to set limits in a democratic fashion.

ACCEPT THE CHILD AS HE IS

The first step in establishing a healthy atmosphere is to accept the child. This does not mean accepting all behavior. It is possible to reject certain behaviors without rejecting the child as a person. Tone of voice and manner must imply that the person is valued even though the present act is not. It is essential to separate the deed from the doer. Consequences must be applied in the spirit of friendliness.

Johnny has put finger marks on the walls. Mother is bothered, but she wants to be respectful. "I see you had an accident; we'll need to take care of this. When will you clean them?"

The ability to accept the child is influenced by several variables. How the parent feels about himself, and circumstances in his life at any given moment, affect his acceptance of the child. Also the specific situation in which a particular behavior occurs influences acceptance; that is, some behaviors that are tolerated when just the family is present may not be acceptable in the company of others.

In addition, some behaviors and some children are easier to accept than others. Parents who attempt to fool themselves with the idea that they feel, or even should feel, equally accepting of all their children often become anxious when they try to accomplish this extremely difficult, if not impossible, task. It's hard to feel loving toward someone who keeps "kicking you in the shins." Parents need to admit this to themselves and stop playing the "I should feel" game. Playing this game keeps the parent in turmoil and hampers the establishment of a more satisfying relationship.

Once parents recognize that acceptance varies, they are in a position to begin increasing their areas of acceptance. This is accomplished through developing a more consistently positive approach to the child. We are not suggesting that the parent become completely consistent, for this would be impossible. We do suggest, however, that one should become aware of the significance of consistency.

It is interesting to note that as you become more accepting of your children they will become more accepting of you. Children who previously "hit you when you were down" become more considerate of your feelings and needs.

Accept that the child is slow in reading or that it is hard for him to get acquainted with people—accept and value him. Don't nag; instead encourage every small positive step.

RESPECT THE CHILD

Essential in influencing anyone toward positive action is respect for the individual. Most of us lack respect for our children. We often talk *to* our children rather than *with* them. Talking to someone implies that he is inferior and automatically shows disrespect. The parent must try to talk with his child in the same manner as he would talk with a good friend.

Also, many of our training procedures with children show disrespect. Parents punish, yell, remind, coax, and generally treat them as inferiors. Often when parents do things for children that they could do for themselves the implication is that they are not capable persons. Parents often make children feel inadequate by criticizing their efforts just because the job is not done as well as an adult could do it. Parents invade their children's privacy by prying into their thoughts and interfering in their affairs.

When dealing with his child a parent can show him respect by taking his feelings and opinions into consideration before acting. When a child feels respected, he himself tends to be respectful and cooperative.

LISTEN, CLARIFY, EMPATHIZE, AND UNDERSTAND

Very few parents know how to truly listen to their children. Often the child begins to tell about an experience or problem and finds the parent either uninterested or lecturing. These responses close avenues of communication. When the parent complains that his child does not share problems with him, it is not difficult to understand why. If the parent were continually tuned out or lectured and admonished by a friend, he would soon stop communicating with that individual. Conversely, as the parent begins to listen and accept the feelings of his child, he will discover that the child will respond.

Dinkmeyer and Caldwell (1970) describe listening skills in terms of the "Art of Conscious Listening." Conscious listening involves an effort on the part of the listener to wait and permit the child to express his inner feelings.

> Deliberately refraining from speaking is difficult. There is always the wish to speak back in reply, to express one's own feelings, to become personally involved, to be conscious of one's own concerns and to take part in the conversation.
>
> But it is actually a very enjoyable experience to simply relax and listen. Discover how truly fascinating people are. Just sit back and let them go. Allow them, without interruption, to express their inner feelings at length. Parents will find this a rewarding way to appreciate and understand their own offspring.

Since many children do not share feelings with their parents because of previous unsatisfying experiences, parents must learn specific techniques and approaches to encourage their children to talk to them. One of the simplest methods is just to lean toward the child. This nonverbal communication conveys to the child, "I am genuinely interested in what you have to say . . . I am prepared to listen." Children will usually respond eagerly to such an invitation.

Verbal invitations can also be offered. The parent can encourage his child to share his problems by inquiring about his feelings, utilizing the "tell me" technique:

"You look upset Billy—could you tell me about it?"

"You look as if you had a bad day, Carol—why don't you tell me about it?"

"You look worried—want to tell me about it?"

The child will recognize the parent's desire to listen, his interest, and his concern. He will feel that his parent really cares.

The parent should be cautioned not to attempt to force the child to share his problems. An overzealous and anxious parent often stifles communication by trying to engage in a sharing experience when the child does not wish to talk. When this happens it is best to drop the subject, but leave the door open:

"I see you don't want to talk about it now, Joey, but if you change your mind I'll be willing to listen and try to understand." A gentle inquiry, a show of concern, interest, and patience usually pay off in time.

When the child decides to talk, the parent must refrain from continually lecturing or preaching. These kinds of responses convey nonacceptance of the child and block further communication and growth. In order to help the child and keep the avenues of communication open, the parent must convey acceptance of the child's feelings, his attitudes, and of the child as a person. When the child is accepted and understood, he feels free of threats and rejection and is in a position to consider alternatives.

As the parent learns to become a more effective listener he will find a warmth, closeness, and cooperative spirit developing that will be highly rewarding to himself as well as his child.

2. *Encourage independence.*

Permitting the child to make his own decisions is difficult for the parent who tends to be overprotective. When a "good" mother proves her worth through service to her child, she resists allowing him to become independent. The more self-sufficient he becomes, the less he will need her and the less essential and worthwhile she will feel.

Inhibiting the child's independence robs him of his security and self-confidence—two necessary and fundamental ingredients for facing life—while encouraging the child to be independent helps give him the freedom to move in ways that permit cooperation and contribution. As an independent individual he will approach his social tasks with the attitude of "What can I offer?" rather than "What will I get out of this?"

To foster independence the parent must permit the child to experiment and develop his capabilities. By trusting his child he can communicate his faith in the child's ability to function. The parent who is interested in promoting this quality looks for every opportunity to encourage independence, refraining from making decisions that are in the realm of the child's abilities. If the child tries to evade independent decisions, the parent can respond with, "It's your problem. I'm sure you can handle it."

As the child grows, there are many opportunities for independent functioning. An infant begins to become independent when Mother learns to allow the child to cry when there is no real need for her service. He soon discovers that Mother does not exist solely to cater to his every whim. As he becomes older he must assume responsibility for his belongings, his room, and he must be allowed to dress and feed himself. When he enters school he becomes responsible for getting up and off to school. Schoolwork also becomes his responsibility. In the child's relations with siblings, peers, and other adults the parent follows a policy of noninterference. In this way the child learns to give and take. The child is given an allowance and permitted to learn how to budget. He is allowed to travel about the neighborhood on his own, to go to the store, movies, and other such places. The child can choose his friends, clothing, and recreational activities. As a teen-ager he becomes responsible for discriminating use of the family car, dating, choosing courses of study, colleges, and professions.

Allowing the child to make his own decisions does not preclude the need for parental guidance. Through friendly discussion the parent can help the child explore alternatives. He will learn to function adequately when he experiences the consequences of his decisions.

3. Avoid pity

One of the most damaging of all human emotions is pity. Feeling sorry for the child, regardless of circumstances, implies that he is weak and robs him of the courage needed to face life. The child who is pitied eventually learns to rely upon self-pity as a way of avoiding difficult situations. He may even attempt to get others to feel sorry for him, hoping that they will solve his problems for him.

There are many situations in which adults find it very difficult not to feel sorry for children. The parents of children with long-term illnesses or handicaps tend to want to make up for these difficulties by becoming oversolicitous. But the handicapped child is hindered much more by parents who pity him than by the physical defect. Such a child must learn to cope with life to the best of his abilities despite his handicap. He needs support and courage to meet life successfully, not pity (Dreikurs and Soltz, 1964).

Poverty, divorce, or the death of a parent are often thought of by parents as traumatic experiences that cause other problems for the child. This belief is highly erroneous. Although these happenings are certainly tragic, they do not necessarily have to be traumatic. The trauma is produced by the way the parents handle the event rather than by the event itself. If the child is pitied, then it is highly likely that he will suffer even into the future. On the other hand, if he is shown empathy, understanding, and support, he will learn to overcome his misery and be able to handle subsequent misfortune.

Help the child face disappointments by recognizing and communicating that he is disappointed, but treat disappointments as a fact of life. When tragedies occur, help him plan ahead instead of dwelling on the tragedy; get him involved, keep him busy. And parents must watch their own behavior, as children look to adults for models when tragedy strikes.

CHANGING YOUR ROLE

The parent can usually change his part in the interaction with the child without changing his basic personality. Most parents do not require psychotherapy, but only need to learn more effective behaviors. Most of us have within ourselves the essential capabilities necessary to change our roles.

When a parent decides to change his approach to his child, he usually goes in all directions at once and creates more problems than he solves. To avoid this trap it is suggested that the parent work on one area at a time.

It is advisable not to attempt to solve your most serious problem in the beginning, because often the area the parent finds the most difficult to change is closely related to his own uncertainty, values, and attitudes (Dreikurs and Grey, 1970). Instead, choose any area where success is likely. For most parents a good place to begin is restricting meaningless talking. Then, when improvement is satisfactory in this area, the parent can move on to another, and so on.

It is interesting to note that as the parent works through problems with the child, other areas of concern begin to correct themselves. For as the parent improves his relationship with his child, the child naturally develops the desire to cooperate.

1. *The desire to change—courage and commitment.*

Changing behavior requires basically two qualities: courage and commitment. If you are courageous and *really* believe what you are reading is what is needed for yourself and your children, then your chances for success are fairly good. If, however, you lack courage, are afraid to fail, or are not certain that this approach is for you, your chances are quite slim. Commitment involves taking specific principles and executing them as consistently as possible.

> Little Harry continually cried each time things did not go his way. His mother usually tried to talk him out of crying with explanations and preaching. This approach usually intensified the crying to the point where Mother would become angry and send Harry to his room.
>
> Mother decided to change her approach. She made a commitment to leave the room whenever Harry began to turn on the "water power." If Mother could not leave the scene, she busied herself with other thoughts or tasks. Before too long Harry stopped his crying jags as he discovered his efforts failed to get his mother involved.

The qualities of courage and commitment lie within each of us and they can be brought to the fore, but we must decide!

2. *Refusing to be overconcerned about what others think.*

Perhaps one of the strongest stumbling blocks to change is overconcern about others. Parents often comment that they would be unwilling to change a certain behavior because of what their neighbors, their child's teacher, or their own parents would think. It is important to recognize that those who look down on an individual are really expressing their own insecurity. If one felt secure, he would have no need to criticize what others do, as long as their behavior did not infringe upon his own rights. When parents realize this, ignoring the opinions of others becomes less difficult. There comes a time for an essential decision: Which is more important to me, the opinions of others or my child's welfare?

THE EFFECTS OF THE REAL ROLE

When parents utilize positive democratic approaches, the results of their efforts are quite different from what is generally produced by authoritarian methods. A child who feels accepted, respected, appreciated, and useful develops feelings of adequacy that influence his attitude and behavior. He enjoys being responsible and becomes interested in cooperation as a means of gaining a sense of belonging. He is generally people-oriented and interested in how he can contribute.

Cooperation and contribution stimulate positive feelings in an individual. It feels good to know one is able to help, and these feelings of usefulness in turn promote more cooperative behavior. A person who feels adequate has social interest and is more concerned with the welfare of the group of which he is a member than with personal gain. His motives are more altruistic than personal. He realizes that he is only one member of the

group and that each person is equal. In the home he is concerned with his total family's happiness and well-being.

A child who is raised in a healthy atmosphere becomes self-
sufficient and independent. He is prepared to meet life and its
demands "standing on his own two feet." He has the courage to
try, and is not afraid of failure. When mistakes are made, he is
not defeated; he is able to pick up and start again. Through his
courage and self-confidence he increases his ability to handle
difficulties and make responsible decisions. Above all, he is a
happy person, enjoying life and all it offers.

THE GENERATION OF GETTERS— STIMULATING THE NEUROTIC PROCESS

1. *Materialism*

The alarming rate at which our technology has grown in the
past several decades has had a definite impact on the mode of
life of adults and children in our society. Our society has become quite materialistic, more concerned with the accumulation of things than with the problems of its members. Success
in life is often measured by how much money and goods a man
accumulates instead of how much he contributes to improving
the welfare of the society.

2. *Bribery*

Parents unintentionally foster the child's overinterest in
"getting" through bribery. How many parents pay their children
for performing household tasks? If payment is not made directly, it is made indirectly through the withholding of allowances for lack of performance. Regardless of the method employed, the child often undertakes work, not in terms of
obligations, but, instead, in terms of monetary rewards. Certainly money is important in life, and people are compensated

for their labors. But there are many necessary tasks for which there can be no monetary remittance. Children must learn to perform necessary household chores as their share in the operation of the home.

In addition, there are some parents who attempt to motivate their children toward greater school achievements through rewards and bribes for grades. This practice is very discouraging to the child, for he often develops the faulty idea that he attends school solely for the purpose of obtaining materialistic rewards rather than for the sake of learning. This approach generally promotes a distaste for learning, as it becomes merely an unpleasant means to an end. Rewards can be unsuccessful if the task seems insurmountable to the child, if the reward is not to his liking, or if he is in rebellion against his parents and views the reward as another attempt to force him. In situations where rewards are effective, parents often find they have to be continually increased to produce desired results.

3. *Spoiling the child.*

Besides rewarding and bribing, many parents spoil their children. This is especially true of parents who feel that as children they missed out because of their own parents' financial problems, or parents who grew up in more affluent atmospheres. These parents often develop attitudes that emphasize accumulation of material goods as a means of gaining status. They like to make certain their children possess as much as or more than the neighbors' children—and thus the goal of "keeping up with the Joneses" rears its ugly head. They often consider their children deprived if they are not at least on equal grounds materially in the neighborhood. Out of their pity these parents buy their children far more toys and other possessions than are necessary.

In addition, parents spoil their children in order to provide further evidence of their own affluence and value. In so doing they distort the child's values, encouraging him to view himself as entitled always to be on the receiving end. He only gives in order to receive. He approaches cooperation with the attitude of "What do I get out of it?" A child who views life and himself this way has difficulty making successful social relationships, as he only knows how to take.

4. *Promoting rebellion.*

The neurotic emphasis on getting has produced many serious problems in our society. Allowing children to believe they can always receive makes them rebellious. Whenever the child feels pressured into doing what he does not want to, or feels deprived of his desires, he rebels—either openly or passively. As a getter, he may seek excitement and pursue pleasure. Some getters turn to abuse of sex and the use of drugs in their rebellion against parents, morality, and society in general.

5. *Focusing on contributions.*

It should be clear that our major task as parents is to work toward developing more healthy attitudes and values in our children. We must help them discover that life consists of both give and take. Our major emphasis should be on the development of social interest. Concern for people must become more important than the pursuit of wealth and prestige.

To accomplish our goal we need to focus on contributions. Our children must learn to give without the ulterior motive of getting.

Give-and-take attitudes can be fostered through the sharing of responsibilities and possessions. At family meetings parents and children plan the division and sharing of necessary household tasks. Through this sharing process children learn cooperation and responsibility. They learn to work together for the good of all, and develop values essential for healthy social relationships.

REFERENCES

Dinkmeyer, Don C., and Charles E. Caldwell. *Developmental Counseling and Guidance: A Comprehensive School Approach*. New York: McGraw-Hill Book Company, 1970, p. 173.

Dreikurs, Rudolf, and Loren Grey. *A Parent's Guide to Child Discipline*. New York: Hawthorn Books, Inc., 1970.

────── and Vicki Soltz. *Children: The Challenge*. New York: Duell, Sloan & Pearce, 1964.

CHAPTER 4

Communication

Perhaps the most essential skill necessary for successful human relationships is communication. If we study people who are successful in life, we generally find effective communicators. They know how to listen to others and how to communicate their own ideas and feelings in nonthreatening ways. They are generally accepting and understanding of the feelings of others.

Watch an effective teacher as she patiently listens and accepts the ideas and feelings of her students. In turn, when she talks, they listen. She is usually successful in influencing them.

Unfortunately, most parents are poor communicators when they deal with their children. They correct, nag, and punish to no avail. In order to influence their children parents must learn how to accept, listen, clarify, understand, and express their own feelings. They must become effective communicators.

TRADITIONAL ROLES PARENTS PLAY WHEN RESPONDING TO CHILDREN'S MESSAGES

Parents characteristically respond in discouraging ways when children send feeling messages. These reponses fit neatly into traditional roles.

The Commander in Chief (ordering, commanding, threatening, controlling):

"Now, listen here, don't you talk to me like that!"

"I said, get busy!"

"Do it—or else!"

"Never mind, you're going to do what I say."

The Moralist (preaching, patronizing):

"That's not the right thing to do."

"You shouldn't do things like that."

"Good little boys don't do those things."

The Know-It-All (lecturing, advising, reasoning, appealing to the child's logic, being superior):

"That just doesn't make any sense."

"If I were you I would . . ."

"Now, you know better than that."

"I've had much more experience than you and . . ."

The Judge (making pronouncements, evaluating):

"You asked for it."

"You didn't do your best."

"Well, if you had studied harder . . ."

The Critic (ridiculing, name-calling, sarcastic, joking):

"You're too big for your britches."

"You're just lazy, that's what."

"Listen here, smarty pants."

"You think you're a big shot around here."

"Ah, come on now, she can't be that bad. I imagine being in a classroom all day with a bunch of little monsters like you would drive her crazy!"

The Psychologist (diagnosing, analyzing, probing, interrogating):

"Your problem is . . ."

"How long have you been worried about this?"

"Okay, tell me exactly what happened."

The Consoler (reassuring):

"Everything is going to be all right."

"All children feel that way at times."

"Don't worry, it's just a stage you're going through—you'll get over it."

Responding to a child's messages in these ways tends to stifle communication. The child may feel defensive, misunderstood, or resentful, and, more than likely, he will stop sharing his feelings. Parents miss many opportunities to help children handle their feelings and to build a good relationship when they rely on these kinds of responses.

RESPONSES THAT KEEP LINES OF COMMUNICATION OPEN

Basic to effective communication is acceptance. Many times lines of communication are severed because individuals, particularly children, will refrain from expressing their true feelings and thoughts for fear of rejection.

Parents have traditionally believed that the way to influence a child is to refuse to accept him. This is a false premise. Because the child so deeply desires acceptance, he will go to great lengths to try to convince the parent of the merits of his behavior. When the parent insists that his attitude is wrong, the child will think of ways to defend it. But if the parent can accept his feelings and help the child express them, he may open the way to a consideration of other alternatives. The child will feel comfortable and understood, and now that he has rid himself of his burden, he can begin to think clearly and explore other methods of meeting his needs more satisfactorily.

It is not enough for the parent to *feel* accepting toward his child. He must express that acceptance. A simple indication by the parent that the child is understood can be sufficient. For example: "I see," "I understand," "I know what you mean." Or the parent can engage in a more complex feedback of what he thinks the child is feeling.

Many times acceptance is communicated through nonverbal clues, such as facial expressions, posture, or gestures. A smile and a pat on the back need no accompanying words, yet they signify acceptance.

Noninterference in an activity in which the child is engaged also demonstrates acceptance. If the child is building a model airplane and the parent does not offer assistance unless his help is sought, he indirectly communicates to the child that his efforts and methods of attacking the project are accepted. In fact, the parent should not be concerned about whether the child is approaching the problem correctly or not. He must allow the child to make his own mistakes and set his own standards. The child's sense of accomplishment and satisfaction is what should be most important to the parent, not the procedure or the product. Interfering in order to show the child the "right" way often conveys nonacceptance by telling the child "you are not capable."

Nonverbal acceptance may simply involve listening. When the parent lets the child talk freely, he indicates by his accompanying nonverbal clues, such as expressions and posture, that he is interested, accepting, and attempting to understand what the child is trying to communicate. The parent indicates by his silence that he genuinely wants the child to share his feelings.

LISTENING SKILLS FOR PARENTS

There are several ways the parent can respond more encouragingly to his child's messages. The "tell me" technique and the "contact" technique are means of eliciting feelings while simultaneously demonstrating acceptance and understanding. The "tell me" technique helps the parent demonstrate his willingness to "tune in" to the child's verbal and nonverbal clues (Dinkmeyer and Caldwell, 1970).

"Sue, you sound as if you're *really* upset—want to tell me about it?"

"John, you look as though you're *quite* worried about something—would you like to tell me?"

When "tuning in" it is best to aim for deep feelings. This way the child can easily modify your interpretation. Whereas if you do not go deep enough, he may think you are unable to understand and will no longer feel inclined to express himself.

The contact technique conveys attentiveness, understanding, and acceptance. The parent maintains contact with the child while he is revealing his concerns and anxieties. The contact technique has basically two dimensions—recognition and reflection. The *recognition* dimension, utilizing responses such as "I see," "Oh?" "I understand," "Yes," "I see what you mean," indicates to the child that the parent recognizes his feelings.

Reflection is a more sophisticated and dynamic aspect of the contact technique. It involves clarification and reiteration of the child's feelings. The parent deciphers the words the child uses, and he reflects what he thinks the child is feeling.

> CHILD: That Jane is such an old rotten brat.
> PARENT: You're *really* angry with Jane.

The child's words are not the true message, they are merely his individual way of communicating his feelings. Reflection serves as a means of checking whether the listener understands what the child is trying to express. If he does not, the child will tell him, and he need only try again.

Reflection also provides a mirror for the child to see himself clearly. He becomes aware of the picture he projects to others. As in television instant playbacks, the child is able to see and understand the impression he creates. After the feedback is received, he can decide whether he likes the image or wants to change it. Such mirroring is termed "reflective listening."

Reflective listening takes practice. To assist parents in their attempts to decode and mirror children's messages we have developed a *feeling vocabulary*. Below is a list of feeling words and phrases that parents can utilize in providing feedback.

Positive Feelings	*Negative Feelings*
happy	unhappy, sad, upset
glad	sad
proud	ashamed

satisfied, pleased	dissatisfied, disappointed, disgusted
everything's working out according to plans	feel as if nothing's going right
sure, certain, determined	confused, worried, puzzled, doubtful
fair	unfair, cheated, feel like getting even, picked on
warmth, warm	distance, distant
respected	worthless, put down
feeling good about self	not happy with self, stupid, jealous
accepted	rejected, left out
courageous, brave	fearful, afraid
secure, confident	insecure, uncertain, lacking faith
adequate	inadequate
comfortable	uncomfortable, mad, angry, annoyed, irritated, hurt
trusted	distrusted, accused
aggressive	shy
important	insignificant, small
excited	bored
honest	dishonest
encouraged	discouraged, defeated, feel like giving up, guilty
sympathetic	indifferent
dependable	can't be counted on
independent	dependent
ambitious	lazy
patient	impatient
like, love	dislike, hate
responsible	irresponsible

When a child sends a feeling message, the parent can utilize the feeling vocabulary to reflect. It is especially important to acknowledge the depth of the feeling by using words like "very," "really," "pretty," "awful."

> CHILD: That Johnny is really mean.
> PARENT: You're *really* angry with Johnny.

CHILD (crying): He broke my doll.

PARENT: You feel *very* sad about that.

CHILD: One of these days I'm going to break something of his.

PARENT: You're mad and you want to get even.

CHILD: I sure do.

PARENT: You feel as though you want to hurt him as he's hurt you.

CHILD: Yes.

CHILD: Dad, look at this model I built.

PARENT: You're *really* proud of it.

CHILD: And I did it all by myself.

PARENT: Looks as if you feel pretty good about being able to do it yourself.

The feeling vocabulary list should not be approached mechanistically. If the parent is only saying words and does not convey his understanding of the feeling, then the child will not feel understood, and he will detect insincerity in his parent's role. Reflective listening must be done in the spirit of mutual respect and in a nonmanipulative manner.

In many cases the child may not reach his own solution during the listening session. Although it is difficult for parents to resist offering suggestions in an attempt to "set him straight," advice will block communication. The child will not feel understood or trusted enough to make his own decisions. Many times, having rid himself of the burden of feelings, the child will find alternatives after the session has concluded. The parent's purpose at this point is just to listen, understand, clarify, and feed back.

Generally the parent should try to make time to listen whenever the child wants to talk for open communication and mutual caring require nourishment. But occasionally the parent may not have time to finish listening to all the feelings the child wishes to express. Rather than leave the child before he has finished, giving him the feeling his parent doesn't care, it is best to arrange an appropriate time to discuss the entire matter.

CHILD: That teacher is so mean! She's going to make all of us stay after school tomorrow just because three kids were talking!

PARENT: You seem *really* angry about this Greg, and I would like to listen to you, but I've got an appointment in a few minutes. Can we talk about this when I come home?

EXPLORING ALTERNATIVE SOLUTIONS

While reflective listening is an effective tool for demonstrating acceptance and understanding and for strengthening the child's problem-solving ability, exploring alternatives is also a valuable way to help the child learn to cope with life's problems.

When the parent permits him to choose and decide he not only treats the child with respect but begins to allow him to be responsible for his own behavior. The fact that it is up to the child, and that the parent believes in his ability to make a good decision, is an important communication. This type of faith undergirds courage.

The problem-solving approach, then, must elicit and help clarify the child's feelings and beliefs.

"You are confused about what to do next; both possibilities are attractive."

It assists by summarizing: "It seems so far you've said . . ."

If there is a block to progress the parent may pose his ideas in a tentative form.

"Is it possible that because . . ."

Or the parent may encourage the child to look at the problem more creatively.

"While you don't know exactly why this is a problem, what would you guess is the reason?"

"Let's pretend this was happening to Tony. Why would it happen to him?"

In some instances the parent can be most helpful by role reversal. Here the child takes the role of the person he is having a problem with and the parent plays the child's role.

When there is a hidden motive or goal not being discussed, and if the relationship is good, the parent might suggest this purpose in a tentative manner: "Could it be you do this, too?"

It is recommended that parents concentrate on developing their reflective listening skills before they attempt to enter into alternative exploration. For if parents move too quickly into this phase, the children may misinterpret their motives as the old methods in a new disguise. However, when the relationship is good, then both the parent and the child enter with all their resources (beliefs, feelings, and experiences), and together they explore uncharted territory. The parent has nothing he is trying to obtain, win, or sell; his entire purpose is to help the child get in touch with his feelings and develop his critical thinking ability.

Sarah comes home crying.

> MOTHER: You seem very upset, Sarah. Want to talk about it? (Recognizing feelings and utilizing the "tell me" technique to encourage dialogue.)
>
> SARAH (crying): The kids at school are always picking on me.
>
> MOTHER: It must be frightening to go to school every day. (Reflective listening.)
>
> SARAH: It sure is, no one likes me. They're always calling me names. I go out on the playground and Joan says, "Here comes Stupid." Then the other kids start to call me Stupid.
>
> MOTHER: What do you do then? (Beginning to explore the interactions to determine how Sarah unknowingly contributes to her problem.)
>
> SARAH: I tell them they're stupid. Joan hits me, and we get into a fight.
>
> MOTHER: How does it end?

SARAH: The teacher stops it and asks us what happened. I tell her about Joan and the others and she scolds them.

MOTHER: Does that end the problem? (Elucidating the failure of Sarah's present method.)

SARAH (sighs): No, it happens over and over again.

MOTHER: Sounds as though you just don't know what to do. (Reflective listening.)

SARAH: Yes.

MOTHER: Why do kids pick on other kids?

SARAH: Because they don't like them.

MOTHER: Why don't kids like other kids?

SARAH: I don't know.

MOTHER: What would be your guess? (Encouraging exploration.)

SARAH: (Shrugs her shoulders.)

MOTHER: Is it possible that kids pick on others because they're fun to pick on? (Posing a hypothesis.)

SARAH: What do you mean?

MOTHER: Well, they get mad, or cry and tell the teacher. (Clarifying.)

SARAH (reflects for a moment): Yes, I guess you're right.

MOTHER: If that's true, then what else could you do when they call you a name? (Encouraging the exploration of alternative solutions.)

SARAH: I guess I could ignore them.

MOTHER: How could you do that? (Exploring Sarah's understanding of the concept of ignoring.)

SARAH: Just walk away and not pay any attention to them.

MOTHER: Okay—but how would you feel inside? (Helping Sarah comprehend the full meaning of ignoring.)

SARAH: I would probably feel mad.

MOTHER: Yes. And remember how we decided that they liked to get you angry. (Reviewing the purpose of the children's teasing.)

SARAH: Yes.

MOTHER: If you decided not to get mad, do you think they might leave you alone? (Helping Sarah realize cause and effect.)

SARAH: Maybe.

MOTHER: Walking away is one way to deal with the problem. Do you think there might be another way? (Summarizing and stimulating exploration of an additional alternative.)

SARAH: What?

MOTHER: Why don't we act out the problem? You play Joan and I'll play you, okay? (Demonstrating a solution through role reversal.)

SARAH: Okay.

MOTHER: You call me names.

SARAH: Here comes Stupid.

MOTHER: Yes, that's right, here I am. Old Stupid is back! (Illustrating the use of an unexpected response that disarms the teaser.)

SARAH: (Dumbfounded, unable to say anything.)

MOTHER: What's the matter? Why did you stop? (Helping Sarah analyze the role-playing.)

SARAH: I don't know.

MOTHER: Is it hard to tease someone who doesn't get upset and just agrees with you? (Posing a hypothesis.)

SARAH: Yes.

MOTHER: How do you feel about that way to handle it? (Encouraging Sarah to express her opinion and any doubts about the alternative.)

SARAH: They would probably laugh at me.

MOTHER: That's true. What could you do then? (Stimulating further problem-solving skills.)

SARAH: I guess I could just laugh with them.

MOTHER: Do you think they might stop eventually if they couldn't get you upset? (Posing a hypothesis.)

SARAH: Yes, I think so.

MOTHER: How could you act toward them at other times, when they're not picking on you? (Exploring a more total approach to the problem.)

SARAH: I could be friendly.

MOTHER: Let's see now, we've discovered two ways to handle the problem—ignoring and agreeing with them. I would suggest you choose one or the other and stick to it. Don't do both or they will just wait to see what you will do next. Do

you want to try out one of these? (Summarizing and pointing out the consequences of inconsistency, Mother leaves the
final decision to Sarah. It is her responsibility to solve the
problem. A commitment is sought.)

SARAH: Yes, I think I'll try agreeing with them.

MOTHER: Let me know how it goes. (Leaving the door
open for further communication if needed.)

THE CONCEPT OF PROBLEM OWNERSHIP

Reflective listening and alternative exploration are skills employed when the child has a problem. In order to recognize
when to use these methods the parent must become familiar
with the concept of problem ownership, or "Whose problem is
this?" The individual upset about the situation is said to "own
the problem."

In parent-child relationships ownership is best determined
by thinking in terms of whose need is not being met.

1. The child has a problem because he is thwarted in satisfying a need. It is not a problem for the parent because the
   child's behavior in no tangible way interferes with the parent's satisfying his own needs. Therefore, THE CHILD
   OWNS THE PROBLEM.
2. The child is satisfying his own needs (he is not thwarted)
   and his behavior is not interfering with the parent's own
   needs. Therefore, THERE IS NO PROBLEM IN THE RELA-
   TIONSHIP.
3. The child is satisfying his own needs (he is not thwarted).
   But his behavior is a problem to the parent because it is
   interfering in some tangible way with the parent's satisfying a need of his own. NOW THE PARENT OWNS THE
   PROBLEM (Gordon, 1970).

Some examples of problems that could be owned by the
child are: uncertainty about career choice, feelings of inade-

quacy, rejection, loneliness, disappointment, frustration, anger, poor school performance, lack of discipline in school, difficulty with homework, conflicts with a brother or sister, difficulty in getting along with peers, and dissatisfaction.

Unfortunately, many parents assume ownership of their child's problems and feel responsible for his behavior at school, with brothers and sisters, peers, neighbors. By assuming ownership of what should be the child's problems, the parent deprives his child of opportunities to learn how to handle problems effectively, hampers his relationship with the child, and decreases his influence. Reflective listening and alternative exploration can help the child become responsible for solving his own problems.

When parents decide to "transfer ownership," that is, to allow the child to take responsibility for the problems he encounters in his life, they can help the child develop problem-solving ability. Transferring ownership does not mean the parent no longer cares about the child, but rather that he cares enough to be concerned about the child's development. He can now accept the child, listen, and demonstrate concern and understanding, but he always realizes that the child is an individual separate from himself who must work out his own problems and learn to "stand on his own two feet."

GETTING CHILDREN TO LISTEN TO YOU

Thus far we have discussed how to listen and respond to children's messages—what to do when the child owns the problem. Now we must look at methods enabling the parent to influence the child. Depending upon the situation, the parent may decide to ignore the misbehavior, utilize natural or logical consequences, enter into problem-solving, or send the child a feeling message.

Unfortunately, when most parents want to tell their children something, they play the same roles they assume when listening—the *Commander in Chief*, the *Moralist*, and so on. Talking to the child in these ways creates "parent deafness." The child tunes the parent out. He doesn't want to hear advice, threats, ready-made solutions, reasons, warnings, or a review of his faults.

The difference between ineffective and effective communication can be seen simply by thinking in terms of "You Messages" and "I Messages" (Gordon, 1970). Most messages sent by parents contain the word "you": "You'd better not do that," "You know better than that," "You'd better stop that," "Don't you think you ought to . . . ?"

If the parent simply tells the child how his behavior makes the parent feel, the message is usually an "I Message." "I can't read when someone is making noise," "I'm worried that I will be late if I have to wait much longer," "I want to take a nap," "I don't like seeing socks and shoes all over the family-room floor." An "I Message" focuses on the parent rather than on the child. Instead of blaming the child, the parent shares his experience.

"I Messages" are generally more effective because, unlike the "You Message," they don't convey disrespect and criticism, and they are less likely to produce antagonism and resistance. They place the responsibility for finding a solution on the child's shoulders. His behavior is interfering with the parent's needs, therefore it is his job to decide what to do about it. "I Messages" convey trust in the child to find appropriate solutions. In addition, the honesty of "I Messages" often influences the child to send honest messages in return.

There are generally three parts to an "I Message":

1. A nonevaluative description of the behavior: "When you leave your bicycle in the driveway . . ."

2. Indication of how the child's behavior specifically interferes with the parent: ". . . I have to move it . . ."

3. The parent's feeling: ". . . and I *really* hate to stop and get out of the car."

Parents can use the feeling vocabulary developed for reflective listening to send their "I Messages."

In using "I Messages" the tone of voice is crucial. If the "I Message" contains tones of hostility the message has the effect of a "You Message," because hostility is an emotion that is aimed at another person. The focus is not on the speaker but rather on the person spoken to. It is best to identify the source of the hostility. Usually it traces back to an initial feeling that was not shared.

> Mr. and Mrs. M. had invited their old friends Mr. and Mrs. J. to play bridge. The evening before bridge night Mr. and Mrs. M. discussed their concern for Mr. J.'s drinking problem and what they should serve during the evening. They finally concluded that they would put all the liquor away and say that Mr. M.'s doctor had advised him not to drink for several months and therefore they simply did not have anything in the house to serve. Mom and Dad were unaware that six-year-old Barry was listening very intently and digesting every bit of information.
>
> The next evening Mr. and Mrs. M. proceeded according to their plan, but Mr. J. foiled them by bringing along a bottle of bourbon as a gift. When Barry came in from playing and saw the drinks he said, "It looks like Mr. J. found that liquor you hid, Dad."

It is understandable that the parents would be angry; however, when either parent decides to talk to the child he will probably be more successful if he identifies the source of his anger as embarrassment and says something like "When you told Mr. J. about hiding the liquor last night, I was embarrassed and afraid that I might lose a friend."

When the parent uses "I Messages" he must be prepared to reflectively listen, for the "I Message" creates a problem for the child. He has to decide what to do about his parent's feeling.

Mother comes home from the store and discovers that ten-year-old Ellen has had other children in the house.

MOTHER: When I come home and find that you have had other children in the house when you agreed not to, I *really* feel let down. ("I Message.")

ELLEN: I'm old enough to look after things, Mom.

MOTHER: You feel I don't trust you! (Reflective listening.)

ELLEN: You don't.

MOTHER: I can see where you might feel that way, but I feel that I *do* trust you. If one of the other children got hurt while I was away I'd be held responsible, and I'd be pretty unhappy about that. (Respecting how the child feels and sending another "I Message.")

ELLEN: Okay.

In many cases the child just wants to be heard, and reflective listening makes him feel understood.

It is essential that the parent realizes the importance of sending "I Messages" about his positive feelings as well. The child benefits from knowing that his parent feels good about him. Such messages help him feel that he is appreciated and loved. In fact, parents must remember to tell their children they love them. Love is often taken for granted, but nothing feels better to a person than to be told that he is loved by someone he cares about. In addition to verbal statements about positive feelings, a smile, a hug, a kiss all express genuine good feeling.

Restrict talking to friendly conversation.

Curbing criticism and restricting talking to friendly conversation often improves family relationships. Tone of voice often indicates how one values the person he is talking to. Many failures in talking with children can be attributed to a harsh or condescending tone.

However, it is not enough just to stop speaking harshly. Many parents shout with their mouths shut! In other words, the parent decides to stop talking about the child's misbehavior, but he continues to *feel* annoyed and angry. His feelings are transmitted to the child through nonverbal clues, such as a frown, tight lips, narrow eyes, brusque manner, and smoldering silence. The child's perception is uncanny. Interviews have demonstrated that even though the parent may be in another part of the house, the child can still know how he feels about his behavior.

Refuse to fight or give in.

The spirit of cooperation is lacking in most homes. Both parents and children view conflicts only in win-lose terms. When conflicts are resolved on a win-lose basis, the loser—whether it be parent or child—usually resents being overpowered by the other, is unwilling to cooperate, and often seeks means of retaliation. Few realize that there is a third way to resolve conflicts—the democratic way. Parents and children can stop fighting and work toward cooperation for mutual benefit.

Dreikurs and Grey (1970) describe four essential principles for resolving conflicts democratically.

1. *Mutual respect:* Each person must respect the rights of the others. Without mutual respect there can be little willingness to cooperate.

2. *Pinpointing the issue:* The issue at hand is rarely the true issue. The true issue is usually of a personal nature, such as prestige, winning and losing, unfair treatment, and rights. Conflicts with children always involve the child's mistaken goals; attention, power, revenge, or assumed inability.

3. *Reaching agreement:* In any human interaction there is always agreement. In a conflict the parent and the child have agreed to fight! However, when one person decides to stop fighting, the other cannot continue the fight. Each person in a conflict usually thinks only about what his opponent should do. Instead, he should think of what *he can do*, thus making a new agreement possible.

4. *Participation in decision-making:* Parents must involve children in the decisions that affect their lives if they wish to

achieve cooperation. There must be full family participation and shared responsibility.

Conflicts can be resolved democratically through natural and logical consequences. The parent removes himself from the position of authority, refusing to fight or give in. Instead he allows the child to experience the results of his misbehavior and assume responsibility for his actions. The child has the option of deciding how he will react to the situation.

> Nine-year-old Richard and his new puppy were playing in the kitchen while Mother was trying to fix dinner.
>
> Mother said, "I'm sorry, but I can't work with this going on. Would you choose to stop playing with the dog, or would you rather play with him outside or in your room?"
>
> Richard replied that he would play with the dog outside. However, in a few minutes he resumed playing with the puppy in the kitchen.
>
> Mother said, "I see you have decided not to play with the dog. We will try again tomorrow."

Instead of becoming angry and ordering her son to leave the kitchen, Richard's mother offered him a choice. Although he agreed to play outside, his behavior indicated that he had really chosen not to play with the dog at all. Mother acted upon his decision and assured Richard he would have another chance.

Some conflict situations require discussion and the exploration of solutions that will be acceptable to everyone involved. But at the time when the conflict occurs it is generally best to withdraw. If both the parent and child are quite emotionally involved, attempts to discuss the issue may degenerate into power struggles. It is generally best to postpone discussion of the conflict until the family meeting, when tempers have cooled and the probability of reaching agreement is increased.

During the discussion of the conflict situation parents can use their reflective listening skills as well as send their own message. Begin the problem-solving session by stating the problem in a friendly, nonjudgmental manner. This is a brainstorming stage, and parents should refrain from evaluating the suggestions. When the children finish, the parents may add their own ideas to the list. Then, by going over the suggestions one at a time, the family can reach a consensus. (See discussion and example of family meeting in Chapter 10.)

Depending upon the nature of the solution, the family may need to seek further agreement on how the solution will be carried out. It should be understood that the decision will be in effect for one week, until the next family meeting, when it can be evaluated. If the children are not following the agreement, the parents may use consequences to demonstrate the necessity of keeping commitments. At the next meeting, when the agreements are evaluated, the parents or the children will have the opportunity to make new suggestions and alter decisions.

The power of the social order

While we suggest discontinuing the use of personal power through rewards and punishments, we stress the importance of establishing respect for order through the use of natural and logical consequences. Consequences differ from rewards and punishments by expressing the power of the social order rather than compliance with the demands of an individual authority.

Time is a natural ally to the parents who utilize the power of the social order to teach the child the need for observance of routine. If a child does not get up on time and is late to school, he may have to make up missed work. A child who comes home late for dinner eats cold food, or, if the family has finished eating, he misses the meal. The child learns to observe time through experiencing the unpleasantness caused by violating schedules. He learns from his own experience. The parent does not command or moralize, but merely acts in a friendly manner.

Natural and logical consequences permit the child to experience the discomforts of lack of respect for order. Natural consequences occur as a result of a violation of the natural order of things. The child who touches a hot stove gets burned. The child who uses a hammer incorrectly may hit his thumb. But he usually learns to be more careful in the future.

If the misbehavior is not governed by natural consequences, or if they are harmful, the parent may arrange a logical consequence. For example, a child who loses a book will have to pay for it. Being careless and spilling a drink results in having to wipe up the table. A child who comes home late from playing cannot go out to play the next day. Fooling around and not getting chores done on time means not watching television until the work is completed.

Consequences must be impersonal, involve no moral judgments, and be applied in a friendly manner. They should deal with what is happening now, and not with past transgressions, and they must offer the child a choice of alternative actions as well as a chance to try again. (For more detailed discussion of natural and logical consequences see Chapter 6.)

SELECTING APPROACHES

We have discussed the following approaches to parent-child problems:

Approach I: Reflective listening and alternative exploration.

Approach II: "I Messages."

Approach III: Problem-solving by reaching agreement.

Approach IV: Natural and logical consequences.

The parent's choice of approach will largely depend upon the situation. Sometimes all approaches may be necessary, while at other times, perhaps only one or two will be needed.

Situations that might involve all the approaches include parent-child conflicts concerning chores, allowance, what time to come home, television and so on. For example, the parent and child may disagree about sharing the chores. The parent voices the problem at a family meeting. It is discussed, using reflective listening and "I Messages," and a final agreement is reached, but not kept by the child. The parent uses natural or logical consequences for the broken commitments. At the next meeting renegotiation takes place, involving more reflective listening and "I Messages," and either a new decision is reached or the family decides to keep the original agreement. If the child still does not keep his agreements, the parents will continue to use consequences.

Many similar situations may be resolved without resorting to the fourth approach—consequences. After renegotiation the child may keep his agreements. In general, as the relationship improves, the parent will find that it becomes less and less necessary to use natural and logical consequences. The child will have more respect for the parent, and he will know that the parent will employ a consequence if necessary. Thus he may decide to modify his behavior before that step would occur.

Reflective listening and alternative exploration are used when the child has a problem or when the parent and the child seek a mutual agreement. However, a warning is due. If reflective listening and alternative exploration are overused, they will provide excess attention and only serve to reinforce the child's purpose. If the child shows no indication of solving the problem through these methods, it may be a clue that the child is using the problem just to gain attention.

> Ten-year-old Jill complained about her teacher. Mother listened, mirroring Jill's feelings. Then they discussed alternatives. But Jill brought the problem home again the next day. Again Mother listened and helped Jill decide what she could do. On the third day Mother decided that Jill had no sincere desire to solve the problem.
>
> When Jill began to cover the same ground again, Mother said, "Jill, we have discussed this same problem for three days, and it appears that you are not quite ready to approach the situation differently. When you decide you *really* want to change your approach, I'll be glad to help."

An alternative response could be the parent's declaration of his inability to help, while at the same time showing faith in the child: "I guess I can't help you with this, Jill, but I'm sure in time you'll figure it out."

"I Messages" also should be used sparingly. Constant reliance on them may trap the parent into giving negative attention, involve the parent in a power struggle, or cause the child to become tired of hearing the parent's feelings—and he may just stop listening altogether.

When an "I Message" fails to produce results, the parent may employ consequences or reach agreement with the child. If the parent decides to use consequences, he must be especially careful not to approach the task with the attitude of revenge: "You don't respect my feelings? Then I'll *make* you do it." He will probably encounter immediate resistance and, in the long run, impede future cooperation. Consequences must be employed in a spirit of friendliness. Like the "I Message," the consequence creates a problem for the child. He must decide how he wishes to respond—whether he wants to remedy the situation or experience the consequences. The parent's interest should be in doing what the situation demands, and not in personal power. Tone of voice and attitude can convey the proper respect for the child.

> Lily is moving a cabinet door back and forth with her foot.
> FATHER: I'm getting concerned that those door hinges will get loose and then the door will not close properly.
> LILY: (Stops momentarily, but starts again.)
> FATHER: I'm sorry, Lily. You can stop doing that or you can leave the room. You decide.

Here the parent sent an "I Message" that was ineffective. He then employed a logical consequence, offering the child a choice in a firm but friendly manner. The child will have to make her decision.

In some situations the parent may rely totally upon consequences. Getting up in time for school is an example. The parent can provide the child with an alarm clock and give him the responsibility for getting up, dressed, to the breakfast table, and to school on time. If he is late he has a problem with the teacher; the parent should not be involved. (This procedure is discussed fully in Chapter 6.) Some other circumstances when the parent should avoid "I Messages" and let the consequences take place are fighting between siblings, doing homework, the child's relationship with his other parent, forgetting, and care-lessness.

In some instances the parent may decide it is best to ignore the misbehavior. Ignoring is a form of a logical consequence, since in order to gain the parent's attention the child will have to alter his behavior. He desires to involve his parent, but can-not do so as long as he misbehaves. The parent demonstrates his willingness to give the child attention only for useful be-havior.

Other practical factors may influence a parent's choice of approach. He may wish to use consequences rather than dia-logue because the misbehavior provides consequences that the parent is unwilling to accept. Timing may be a factor. Early in the morning the parent may not have time to respond with "I Messages." The parent's physical condition may make discus-sion too uncomfortable. There may be points of extreme con-flict that need immediate attention. Or previous experience with dialogue in these situations has proved to be ineffective.

Be creative—act, don't react.

The parent's reaction to misbehavior often reinforces it. Instead of reacting, the parent must act. If the child uses mis-behavior to gain attention, don't nag, threaten, or criticize. Depending upon the situation, the parent can ignore the misbe-havior, or give attention in ways the child does not expect through reflecting, sending "I Messages," or using logical con-sequences. If the child tries to overpower him, the parent should withdraw and let the consequences occur.

The misbehaving child counts on his parent's "normal" reaction to achieve his goal. Don't become trapped, do what he does not expect!

Rules are for parents too.

Lack of respect for family rules is a common problem. Rules are usually established by parents and handed down in dictatorial form to their children. Parents then expect to be able to violate their own rules while still requiring obedience from their children. Problems arise when the child's resentment of the unilateral rule-making erupts into rebellion and misbehavior. The child should participate in making decisions that affect him.

Once the rules are agreed upon, the parents as well as the child are obligated to observe them. There can be no double standard. For example: If the family has decided to share responsibilities, the child will expect the parent to participate in the chores. Many fathers feel that it is unmanly to do household duties. They insist this is women's work, or try to reason that since they work all day they should not be required to share the burden of home tasks. But these men forget that their wives also work hard all day raising the children and managing the household. They forget that their children, too, have put in a full day's work! School and play are the child's occupation, the work he must do in order to mature. Rules, then, must apply to all members of the family. No member can be privileged if the family expects cooperation.

Listen; children have good ideas.

Adults almost universally believe they have all the solutions to daily problems. The parent fails to solicit and listen to his child's ideas, for, after all, he, the parent, is more experienced and therefore knows what's best. But children often do have good ideas, and listening to them with a receptive mind is a necessary ingredient in any satisfactory parent-child relationship.

The family had acquired a new puppy. Father was attempting to paper-train the dog. Whenever he caught the pup after he had made a mess on the floor he would scold him and place him on the paper.

One day nine-year-old Jim saw Dad disciplining the dog.

> JIM: Dad, maybe if we watch him right after he eats, we will catch him about to go. Then we could put him on the paper, and after he finishes we could tell him that he was a good dog and give him a puppy biscuit. Maybe then he would learn.
>
> DAD: You know, that sounds as if it might work. Let's try it.

Jim and his father made an agreement to take turns watching the pup. It was not long before the pup learned what was expected of him. Both Dad and Jim were pleased with their accomplishment.

Keep your control.

When the parent starts to change his role, he may notice that the child is actually becoming more difficult. This is not unusual. For example, a child who has always gotten his way by staging temper tantrums is not willing to discontinue immediately after they begin to fail. He will test the parent, his tantrums worsening as he attempts to force a reaction. This is a sign that the parent's change of behavior is having an effect. During this difficult period the parent must not lose his self-control. If necessary, he should go into another room, or take a walk, returning only when he feels he can control himself. Then, if corrective actions are necessary, he can effect them in a friendly way. When the child realizes his behavior will only cause the parent to leave, he will alter his behavior. Performing is not effective without an audience.

HAVE COURAGE

Sometimes parents try to change their approach to children, and after the first few attempts have failed, they give up. They forget that their own and their children's present behavior were not learned overnight and that it will take time to unlearn them. Parents must have patience not only with their children but with themselves. Mistakes should be learning experiences. How can the situation be approached differently the next time? Each day offers another chance. Parents must tackle their task courageously, accepting their errors. If, instead, parents allow themselves to become discouraged by mistakes, if they feel these testify to their inadequacy as parents, they cannot profit from them.

There is no such thing as a perfect parent. Relax and be human; children will accept their parents' imperfections. The parents' example of patience, mutual respect, and acknowledgment of their own mistakes will teach more than any attempt at perfection.

REFERENCES

Dinkmeyer, Don C., and Charles E. Caldwell. *Developmental Counseling and Guidance: A Comprehensive School Approach*. New York: McGraw-Hill Book Company, 1970.

Dreikurs, Rudolf, and Loren Grey. *A Parent's Guide to Child Discipline*. New York: Hawthorn Books, Inc., 1970.

Gordon, Thomas. *Parent Effectiveness Training*. New York: Peter H. Wyden, Inc., 1970.

CHAPTER 5

Encouragement

One of the most important topics in this book is encouragement. Unless parents can develop the skill to encourage, they will not be effective in their child-training efforts.

Too often parents harbor an idealized mental image of what their child should be and how he should perform. But it is important to recognize that none of the standards, values, and goals we set for the child can be achieved until he himself feels adequate and self-satisfied. The child can only function as an effective human being after he believes in himself. Mistakenly, parents spend considerable time attempting to locate the child's weaknesses and liabilities, and then proceed to try to eliminate them. As with many things, their intentions are good; it is only their methods that are inappropriate and ineffectual.

We must recognize that we can never change a person's behavior unless we first change his expectations. There is considerable power in our interpersonal relations with children. Too often we use it inappropriately. We indicate to children both verbally and nonverbally: "I guess you won't make it"; "I suppose it's too hard for you"; "That's not the right way—I'll do it for you."

Fred, age nine, has been assigned two jobs, making his bed

and setting the table. He seldom cooperates, and his mother openly complains to his father, "Fred can't be counted on to do his jobs; I usually have to do them for him." The message Fred receives is "I'm not dependable," and the consequence is "If I fail to function Mother will do it for me."

The misbehaving child is always a discouraged child. Fred does not believe he can find his place in the family or feel adequate by behaving properly. His faulty assumptions and private logic tell him that if he misbehaves, at least he will be noticed and not ignored. His parents' goal, then, must be to build Fred's self-esteem, his courage to try, and his feeling of adequacy, so that he will believe in himself and be willing to make an effort.

Encouragement means an almost unlimited acceptance of the child. It identifies all of his assets and strengths. It refuses to become overconcerned with his liabilities. Encouraging parents are pleased with a full and complete effort, but they are equally pleased to recognize any partial, positive effort on the part of the child. Encouragement is based upon a belief in the innate capacity of man to overcome the challenges of life if he has the support of those who are important to him.

The encouragement approach requires that parents be courageous. Anyone reading a book about child psychology, purposes of behavior, and the games children play will often see himself as the victim, the ineffective one, the frustrated adult. As he reads he will find his own errors on many pages. However, the purpose in pointing out mistakes is not to fault the parents, but rather to help them understand their mistakes and to indicate ways in which they can change. But even if a parent changes, he must realize that he will not be the "perfect parent." He must have the courage to recognize that many times after a particularly difficult incident he will sit back and reflect, "That probably was the worst way to handle the situation." However, the way in which the parent deals with his own mistakes has much to do with his effectiveness. In essence, the parent cannot encourage a child until he can accept himself and has begun to build his own self-respect and his self-esteem as a parent.

DISCOURAGEMENT

In order to properly understand the place of encouragement in child training, one must know the significance of discouragement. Discouragement is always based on one's evaluation of himself in a situation. A discouraged self-evaluation occurs when a person does not feel adequate, and as a result, possesses limited courage. He feels fearful and doubts his ability to handle a situation. These beliefs and attitudes will influence his future interaction with others.

The discouraged child believes that he has little possibility of solving his problems, or even of moving toward a solution. He lacks confidence and approaches each challenge with the anticipation that he will perform poorly or fail. One begins to recognize that the convictions underlying discouragement are based on faulty overconcern with status and prestige. If the child is preoccupied with a need to be in a position that is superior to the positions of others, then obviously he will regularly be discouraged and dissatisfied. The antidote for discouragement begins with the courage to be imperfect, the acceptance of one's limitations and failures. This means that the parent must help the child identify natural human imperfections and learn how to live with them.

It is the parent's duty to know the nature of the forces within the family atmosphere and the family constellation that stimulate discouragement. These forces include:

1. *Too high standards:* The setting of an increasingly difficult standard makes success impossible and discourages the child; for example, the child who gets all C's on a report card is now expected to get all B's; the child who gets all B's is now

expected to get all A's; the child who plays the piano reasonably well is now expected to become an artist.

2. *Sibling competition:* Parents, often unintentionally, pit the siblings against each other by comparing the excellent performance of one with the poor performance of another. Siblings have a significant impact upon each other, and in our culture the social competition between them brings about severe discouragement.

3. *Overambition:* In our culture overambition is a product of faulty standards and a major, but seldom recognized, deterrent. Overambition is displayed by all those who give up when they cannot excel. If one carefully examines what appears to be a preference for certain activities, it becomes clear that this is more the result of discouragement in other areas than an actual free choice. In other words, some children become extremely talented in music as a result of their frustration in competing in athletics or academics. This type of compensation has its advantages, of course, but we would stress that the child ought to be able to courageously accept that he can try even if he isn't outstanding.

Overambition can be observed in the child who, because he does not play ball skillfully, refuses to join the game. Then, because he cannot excel constructively, he may switch to excellence in rebelliousness, or he may become "the biggest nuisance," "the most passive student I have ever had," or "the shyest child in the family." These are the products of overambition and a competitive culture that values position and status more than persons.

METHODS OF ENCOURAGEMENT

Our typical methods of child training focus upon overprotection, keeping the child dependent, setting unrealistic standards, and stimulating competition. These factors are almost guaranteed to produce a discouraged child. Instead, the parent must learn to talk less and to completely discontinue making negative comments about the child as a person. Of course there will be times when he will be displeased with the child's actions. However, the parent must always make it clear to the child that while he does not approve of his action, he still approves of him as a person. In effect, the parent communicates: "I don't like what you are doing although I like you."

The basic methods of encouragement include the following precepts:

1. *Value and accept the child as he is.*

We can build security only as we sincerely value the total person. This means accepting the child just as he is, with all his faults. Although parents believe they are valuing him, and may actually be stating this to the child, often their nonverbal cues, such as tone of voice, actions, expressions, or even a glance are signals to the child that he is not living up to his parents' expectations.

It is vital to separate the deed and the doer. When the child does not perform in the way his parents had expected, they must help him understand that his failure was due to a lack of readiness or ability, but that in no way does this reduce his value as a person.

Billy has been playing Little League baseball. Father is very ambitious athletically and has spent a lot of time helping Billy learn to hit and field. He seems to do well when father is practicing with him, but during games he becomes extremely nervous. After one game in which Father watched him strike out twice and make several fielding errors Billy and his father were extremely discouraged.

Father should separate the deed from the doer. He must take the time to point out the good aspects of Billy's plays, the balls he did field, the valuable part that he played in the general teamwork.

BILLY: We really got bombed in that game, and I was the worst one.

FATHER: You feel it was a very poor game.

BILLY: Not only that—I was no good.

FATHER: I guess it seems as if nothing went right—but remember, this is your first year.

BILLY: I'll never be a star like Jack.

FATHER: Maybe not, but you did field several balls well, and you hit a good solid drive to second base.

BILLY: Will you still practice with me?

FATHER: Certainly—it's fun for both of us.

Sometimes when discussing a child's performance with him, the parent can stress that he is pleased with him as a person by stating something such as, "You made some mistakes, son, *but* look at the way you . . ." This technique of turning the "but" around lets him know that it is okay for him to make mistakes and that his parent's real interest is in what he accomplished successfully. This, incidentally, will be quite different from the faint praise many receive *before* a "but" that introduces the complaint.

2. *Use words that build the child's self-esteem and feeling of adequacy.*

Parents seldom recognize how significant their verbal interactions with children are. The parent has considerable capacity and countless opportunities to build the child's feelings of self-respect and adequacy by indicating his pleasure in any accomplishment or effort of the individual. When the child is facing a particularly difficult task, the parent can help him prepare for the task by leaving him with the attitude that the parent feels "You can do it." Even if he is not completely successful, the parent should make sure the child knows he has not slipped in his estimation.

Often children will be in school recitals, contests, or athletic events where parents attend. At times when the child does not

meet with success, the parent should relay some of the following attitudes to his child:

I was really pleased to be there and be your parent.

I am glad you played and participated.

While everything didn't come off as you hoped, I felt it was
a very good try.

I can see you have made lots of progress since your last
effort.

Everybody makes mistakes. They help you learn.

Science has enabled us to inoculate the child against a large
variety of diseases. There is no such magic formula to protect
against failure and unhappiness! Parents who apply the concepts in this book can build the child's security and self-
confidence.

3. *Show faith in the child so he can believe in himself.*

The child must feel that he is an important member of the
family and is worth more than any of the problems that he
may become involved in. For example, in times of economic
troubles, parents may complain about what it costs to feed,
clothe, or school a child. This may cause the child to wonder if
he is really valued, in light of all the complaining.

Parents often hold the child's past failures against him. He
comes to feel prejudged. From his point of view, there is no
way to change his reputation. Parents say, "I know that the last
time you had a dog you didn't walk him, so I don't think we
can get you one again"; or "When you tried dancing class you
lost interest, so I don't think I'm going to be able to support
guitar lessons."

In many instances the parent must forget past failures. Instead, he must help the child believe in his own capacities.
And this means the parent must have the courage to permit
the child to start with a clean slate. He may remember the
child's past successes, but he must never burden him with a
record of his past mistakes. Remember, whenever the parent is

trying to change the child's motivations, he is involved in attempting to change his anticipations and expectations. However, his anticipations will not change if the parent is already so discouraged that he believes that the child will fail to function.

Sometimes parents are so cautious with their material things that they underrate their child's capacity to function. For example, Mother buys new china dishes, instead of plastic. Now she is not willing to let Janet help her with the dishes. She explains that they should wait until Janet is a little older and less likely to break them. Janet's mother must consider whether it is more important to have broken dishes or damaged courage. Our observation indicates that broken dishes can be repaired and replaced much more easily than rebuilding a child whose courage is broken.

4. *Plan for experiences that are guaranteed to give success.*

Planning for success may mean modifying standards so that success is always feasible. In the family meeting parents should give some attention to planning learning experiences within the family which enable the child to develop a self-concept of being adequate and successful. For example, the parent can help the child select the tasks that he feels the child wants to do and will be able to do well, thus giving him regular opportunities to demonstrate his competency and success. While a child can learn from the natural consequences of a mistake, it is equally important to plan successes that will create for him an image of self-confidence.

DIFFERENTIATING PRAISE AND ENCOURAGEMENT

Often encouragement is confused with praise and reward. While praise may be of value, it can also be discouraging if the child maintains a low opinion of himself or becomes dependent on this external reward. Praise is like a reward for something well done, and implies a spirit of competition. The unspoken message is clear: "The spoils to the victor." Praise may make members of the group who are unpraised unwilling to try. And the child who sees a sibling praised while he is ignored is often permanently discouraged in that particular area.

John, eleven, and Billy, ten, were returning from their tennis lesson.

> MOTHER: Billy, you really hit the ball well today.
> BILLY: But my backhand wasn't very good.
> MOTHER: It was much better than last week. John, didn't Billy do well?

This type of exchange, which does not include positive comments for John, may cause John to abandon his efforts in tennis. Praise is based upon external evaluation and must be continually earned. Although the child likes to receive praise, he is never sure when he will get it again. In addition, he may come to expect praise and thereby fail to function when it does not occur.

In contrast to praise, encouragement may be given for any effort or for slight improvement. And while praise may make the child feel special, encouragement is not concerned with superior-inferior relationships but focuses on helping the child feel worthy. The benefits of encouragement are long-range but lasting. Self-confidence and self-respect give the child the courage to accept the challenges life offers.

THE LANGUAGE OF ENCOURAGEMENT

Our autocratic tradition, emphasizing punishment and reward, has trained us to prod and nag rather than encourage. Often our language merely echoes the comments our own parents made to us. We must learn new words and phrases if we are to be effective in changing the child's view of himself.

However, encouraging language cannot hide a negative basic attitude, for the child is readily able to detect insincerity and pretense. If the parent sincerely values the child just because he is human, with both potential and liabilities, encouragement will flow freely. This approach to parent-child relationships brings joy to the parent as well as to the child.

The parent's conversation should focus on recognition of effort rather than on accomplishment. This places a value on the child as he is, not as he could be. This type of communication will stimulate the child's capacity to see the positive, and eventually it will influence his own vocabulary and communication processes.

The contrast between encouragement and words that discourage and do not foster growth can be exemplified as follows:

Words That Encourage	Words That Discourage
Knowing you, I'm sure you will do fine.	Knowing you, I think you should do more.
You can make it.	You usually make mistakes, so be careful.
I have faith in you.	I doubt that you can do it.
Thanks for your help.	If you had finished clearing the table, that would have been helpful.
You're doing fine.	You can do better.
I enjoyed that song.	Your music is getting better, but you missed the notes at the end.
I can see you put a lot of effort into that.	That is a good job, but the corners are ragged.
You have really improved!	Well, you're playing a little better than last year.
You'll figure it out.	You had better get some help, that looks very difficult.
You can only learn by trying.	I doubt you should try.
That was a good effort; don't worry about the mistake.	Why didn't you think of that before you started?

Let's think this through together.	How can you be so dumb?
You've done some good thinking. Are you ready to start?	That plan will never work.
That's a challenge, but I'm sure you'll make it.	That is too difficult for you. I'll do it.

The difference between discouragement and encouragement is often very subtle, as it is affected by the perceptions and the courage of the child. For example, in a good relationship the child can perceive the parent's intent as positive even though his words may be critical and appear to be discouraging.

DETERRENTS TO ENCOURAGEMENT

The challenge to build an encouraging relationship with the child is an awesome one, particularly to those of us who were raised in the autocratic tradition, which placed an overemphasis upon excellence and being more than others. This orientation has caused us to consider deficiency and failure to comply as violations of the demands and obligations of society. The democratic approach to human relationships does not expect more of a child than he can produce.

We must recognize that by nature and tradition we are better equipped to find fault, humiliate, and demand. Fault-finding and humiliating behaviors occur most typically when we feel that our status and prestige are threatened. We are most inclined to discourage when we feel the child is spoiling our self-image. Thus as adults we must look at our own competitive relationships with people within our family and community. Do we feel that our child must be a product that makes us look good? Are we overconcerned with being the best parent? In order to see the child's assets, we must build a new, optimistic relationship, based on the adult's courage to be imperfect and satisfaction with his own progress as a parent. Our children will not develop the courage to be imperfect unless they have examples to emulate.

PART II

RESPONSIBILITY WITHOUT PUNISHMENT

CHAPTER 6

Learning Respect for Order Through Experience and Consequences

DEVELOPING RESPONSIBILITY IN CHILDREN

All parents would agree that adequate preparation for life requires a sense of responsibility. Few know how to foster responsibleness, however. Commonly it is felt that one must "teach" responsibility. Punishment, rewards, and bribes are the tools of the "teaching" process. These methods are generally unsuccessful, as a parent cannot "teach" responsibility, he must give it to the child and let him learn how to handle it.

There are basic rules involved in helping children assume responsibility.

1. *Avoid performing tasks a child can do for himself.*

This rule is often violated by parents who have high standards and treat their children as if they are incapable of meeting them. When a child is first learning to assume responsibility he may not conform to adult standards. The product is not as important as the effort. Children often become discouraged and refuse to accept responsibility if parents are not accepting of their efforts. Allow the child to help at every opportunity. Assist the young child to take responsibility for dressing him-

self, keeping his room orderly, taking care of his personal belongings, helping set and clear the table.

2. *Allow time for training.*

Many attempts to develop responsibility fail because of poor
timing. The worst time to train a child is when there are definite time limits involved. A relaxed time is the best time to
train a child. The parent is under no pressure and can be patient and encouraging. For example, attempting to train a
young child to tie his shoes in the morning when Mother is
rushed invites failure. If pressure of time wears on Mother's
patience, she is apt to be critical and try to push the child, or
she may eventually give in and do it for him. The child is likely
to become discouraged and refuse to cooperate.

3. *Ask—don't demand.*

Making demands on children usually decreases their desire
to help out. On the other hand, requesting their cooperation
by emphasizing the parents' need for assistance and their ability to provide it is appealing to many children. The child feels
grown up as he discovers he is of real help to his parents. "Bill,
this job is difficult and I sure need your help, will you help me
please?" If the child refuses, this is usually a clue that the relationship is not as it should be. Therefore it is best to accept his
denial and continue to work on improving the relationship. At
the times the child does help, show appreciation. "Thanks,
Bill, you made my job much easier."

4. *Use natural and logical consequences.*

When a child refuses to perform those tasks which are his
sole responsibility, the parent needs to stop talking, withdraw
from conflict, and let the child experience the consequences of
his irresponsibility. No one would learn to become responsible
if others continually took the responsibility for them. As long
as parents perform the child's duties, he will not become responsible. In succeeding chapters the parent will discover

many natural and logical procedures designed to help children learn to assume responsibility.

As children learn to accept responsibility they begin to enjoy being responsible. They gain confidence and feel worth while. Occasional periods of discouragement can be counteracted by reminding them of success in previously performed tasks.

ESTABLISHING RESPECT FOR ORDER

Observing the rules of order holds top priority in any established society, for without order, chaos and eventual self-destruction can be the only course. Each parent has an obligation to train his child to observe the order of our society to insure its survival. Unfortunately, the child-raising methods currently at the parent's disposal are so antiquated that he often fails. Permissiveness and autocratic methods alike have raised children who have difficulty accepting order, little respect for authority, and who are concerned only with their own rights. These children must experience the inconvenience of disorder before they can recognize authority and the restrictions it imposes as beneficial and vital.

When a parent continually tries to force his child to wear his coat in cold weather, the child resists. He resents the parent's authority. And if he wears his coat at all, the child may remove it when he is out of his parent's sight. But when his parent stops arguing and reminding him and allows the child to experience the discomfort of going without a coat, he soon learns the necessity of observing this rule. The next time his parent suggests he wear a coat, his chances of gaining the child's cooperation are greatly increased. The child accepts the suggestion because it is personally beneficial, not just because his parent demands it.

In order to resolve conflicts effectively we must approach them through democratic procedures. *Natural* consequences, such as the discomfort of going without a coat in cold weather, provide a method for the parent to allow the child to learn from the natural order of events. The parent does not threaten the child, argue, or concede, but rather he permits the child to discover on his own the advantages of respect for order. He replaces stimulation from without with stimulation from within. By experiencing consequences the child develops a sense of self-discipline and internal motivation. He respects order not because he will be punished otherwise but because he has learned that order is necessary for effective functioning (Dreikurs and Soltz, 1964).

Many child-training experiences are not governed by natural consequences or else allowing the child to experience such consequences would be dangerous or harmful. In such cases the parent must develop logical consequences to fit the situation. He must be careful not to confuse consequences with punishment.

> Logical consequences are arranged by an adult but must be experienced by the child as logical in nature.
> 1. Logical consequences express the reality of the social order, not of the person; punishment, the power of a personal authority.
> 2. The logical consequence is logically related to the misbehavior; punishment rarely is.
> 3. Logical consequences imply no element of moral judgment; punishment often does.
> 4. Logical consequences are concerned only with what will happen now; punishments, with the past.
> 5. The voice is friendly when consequences are invoked; there is danger in punishment, either open or concealed. (Dreikurs and Grey, 1970).

The best consequence can be turned into punishment through misapplication. Anger, threats, warnings, reminding may destroy the effect. In some instances the parent may not verbalize her feelings but communicate a punitive attitude nonverbally; she essentially "shouts with her mouth shut."

Mrs. Z. had a problem with ten-year-old Becky. Each w day she would have to prod Becky to put her dirty clothes the clothes hamper.

Mrs. Z. had heard about logical consequences from her neighbor, and she decided to try this new approach. She told Becky that she would wash each Monday and that she would wash only what was in the hamper.

Becky "forgot" to put her clothes in the hamper. She created a pile of dirty clothes on her bedroom floor and just kept adding to it. Throughout the week her mother would hint, "Don't you think you should pick up your dirty clothes?" or "Remember I said I will only wash what is in the hamper."

Monday came and Becky still had not put her dirty clothes in the hamper. Consequently, nothing of hers was washed. The next morning Becky complained that she didn't have any clean school clothes to wear. Her mother replied, "Since you didn't put anything in the hamper, I guess you'll have to wear your old clothes." Becky grumbled some more and finally put on an old outfit.

Another week went by and Becky still did not put her dirty clothes in the hamper, although her mother reminded her several times. Then when Monday morning came her mother lost her patience. Angry and frustrated, she demanded that Becky put her clothes in the hamper.

Mrs. Z. complained to her neighbor that logical consequences had not worked.

Mrs. Z.'s consequence was ineffective because she did not remain firm in her decision. She coaxed, reminded, and finally gave in. Through her irresponsibility Becky gained control, keeping her mother involved with reminders and threats. In addition, Becky had no need to assume the responsibility for getting her clothes washed, for her mother herself took the responsibility, first through her comments and finally by commanding Becky to put her clothes in the hamper.

If Mrs. Z. had stated her intentions concerning washday and refrained from all subsequent comments, and if she had allowed her daughter to experience the consequences of her irresponsible behavior, Mrs. Z. probably would have gained results. When Becky complained about having nothing to wear Mrs. Z. should have placed the total responsibility on Becky's shoulders by saying something like "I'm sure you'll figure out what to do." This conveys her faith in Becky's ability to solve the problem and does not give the issue or the child any unwarranted attention.

Consequences can also be spoiled by hidden motives. They must be applied in a friendly manner with no strings attached. The parent permits the child to choose and accept the responsibility of his choice. Children usually learn to do what the situation demands because they see value in certain kinds of responses. If, however, the parent uses the consequences with the intention of forcing the child to give in to his wishes, if he is unwilling to accept the child's own choice, or if he attempts to manipulate through the consequence, the child will perceive this. Instead of positive change in behavior and lasting results, the child will respond with fortified resistance.

> "Billy, we will eat at six o'clock. If you wish to eat supper, you will have to be home around that time." (Billy has been given the option of coming home on time to eat supper or not, as he chooses.)
> Billy tests his mother by coming home after the dishes have been cleared.
> "Where's dinner, Mom?"
> "I'm sorry, Billy, but you decided not to come home in time for supper. I'll fix you a good breakfast in the morning."

The effect of this approach is very different from being told, "Billy, you're late again. You can go straight to bed without your supper!"

With the exception of being sent to bed, the same result occurs—hunger. Since his mother had given him a choice, and then upheld her decision without moralizing or becoming angry, Billy has a good chance of learning a lesson. If she had become upset or not given him a choice at all, she would have invited retaliation, and no learning would have taken place.

When applying a consequence it is very important to stay friendly and nonretaliatory. Like the mother in the example above, each parent must show the child that he is interested in helping him, not in making him "pay for his crime." Although we have no guarantee of how the child perceives our actions, we have a much better chance of success if we make him aware that we do not enjoy his suffering. When the parent is angry and upset the child often feels that the parent is rejecting him as a person. But when the parent continues to be friendly, the child senses that he is valued, even though his behavior is not.

The old saying "Experience is the best teacher" is often paid lip service but seldom put into practice. Most of our disciplining is done by coaxing, reminding, threatening, and punishing, rather than by simply allowing children to experience the unpleasantness of their actions. While we may believe we are protecting the child, in truth we are denying him a learning experience. Logical consequences make sense to the child because they are what he might expect to happen without our interference.

Mike, age ten, and his father, were building a model airplane together. Mike was eager and started right away to try to put pieces together. Father said, "Mike, I think we can do a much better job if we read the instructions first." Mike verbally agreed, but began to glue some pieces in place while his father patiently read the instructions. Father refrained from comment and let Mike attack the problem in his own way.

A half hour later Mike had completed the model except for one piece. Mike tried to put the piece in its place but found that it would not fit.

"Why won't this darn thing fit?" wondered Mike out loud. Father made no reply. Mike looked puzzled and turned to his father, "Dad, why can't I make this fit?"

"I think it's because that part had to go in before the piece marked '14.' "

"Oh no," sighed Mike. "Can it be fixed, Dad?"

"I'm afraid not, son, the glue has already dried."

Mike appeared sad as he looked at the ruined model.

"You seem pretty upset about this," said Father.

"I am," said Mike.

"I know you were looking forward to hanging this up in your room. I'm sure it's pretty disappointing."

"It sure is," replied Mike.

"What do you think we could do the next time to prevent this from happening?" asked Father.

"I guess we'd better follow the directions," sighed Mike.

Here Father did not lecture on the virtue of following directions. He made his suggestion, and Mike chose to ignore it. Father let him discover the value of instructions through experience. He used reflective listening to show Mike he understood how it felt to ruin a project, and he helped Mike learn to avoid the error in the future without being smug and saying "I told you so."

In order for consequences to be effective parents should follow a procedure that is consistent.

1. *Verbal choice*: "David, you may settle down and watch TV with us or leave the room. You decide."

2. *Implementing the child's decision*: Child settles but acts up again. "I see you have decided to leave. Come back when you are ready to settle down."

When encountering resistance—as when the child refuses to leave—"Do you want to leave on your own or should I help you?" If the child does not go, he has decided to leave with help. Firmly but kindly remove him.

3. *Repetition of same or similar behavior at another time*: "I see you have decided to leave. I'll come and get you when you are ready." If he does not go, assume he has decided to leave with help and remove him. Go to get him in about fifteen minutes. "You may come back now." If he decides not to come, leave him.

At succeeding occurrences of the misbehavior say nothing,

just remove him. Go to get him in about one-half hour. Increase the amount of time on each repeat of the misbehavior.

A TYPICAL DAY IN FAMILY LIFE

Difficulties often arise out of the daily routine, presenting particularly annoying and recurrent problems for both parents and children. Rather than become increasingly frustrated day after day, the parent can put an end to routine disturbances by employing consequences.

Rush hour

Mothers often report that getting the children up, dressed, fed, and off to school is a daily struggle. The children refuse to get up, and then they fight and argue at the breakfast table.

> Mrs. J. has two boys, Tom, ten, and Steve, six. Every morning was bedlam. Tom would have to be called several times before he would finally get up. Steve would get up on the first call, but then he would constantly cry for his mother's help in picking out his clothes and in getting dressed. Both boys argued during breakfast. They refused to eat whatever their mother had prepared and forced her to provide something different. Many times, because of all the fuss, the boys missed the bus and their mother had to drive them to school.

This mother is a victim of two very powerful boys who treat her like a slave. Mrs. J. believes that she is responsible for getting her sons off to school. She fails to see how she is depriving them of the necessary experience of learning to be on time. If she continues her present methods, her sons may never learn this lesson.

Mrs. J. has to begin to place the responsibility for "rush hour" where it belongs. First, she should provide the boys with alarm clocks, teach them how to set their clocks, and inform her sons that she feels they are by themselves capable of getting up, dressed, fed, and off to school. Steve will have to assume the responsibility of picking out his clothes and getting dressed on his own. Tom will have to get out of bed when his alarm clock sounds.

Breakfast should be placed on the table. Mrs. J. will call the boys once, and give them the choice of eating what is available or not eating, as they prefer. If they refuse to eat, they will experience the natural consequence of being hungry.

If the boys miss the bus, they will have to walk to school and experience the logical consequence of being late. It may be helpful for Mrs. J. to call the teacher and inform her of what she is trying to do, asking for her cooperation in seeing that the boys make up time and work missed.

Mrs. J. must remain firm in her decisions and refrain from reminding, coaxing, nagging, or "shouting with her mouth shut." She must be willing to allow her sons to experience the consequences of being late. After two or three days the boys will probably learn the value of being on time.

If busy, unguarded traffic intersections and other obstacles make it inadvisable to let the children walk to school, an alternate approach may be used.

Stuart, age six, always dawdled in the morning, forcing his mother to get him up, dress him, and rush him out the door just in time for the school bus. Mother decided that it was time Stuart learned to be responsible for getting himself off to school. She bought him an alarm clock, taught him to use it, and informed him that it was his responsibility to catch the bus in time for school.

The next morning Stuart overslept and missed the bus. He began to cry, wondering what to do. Mother said, "I guess you will have to stay home, and the only reason for staying home from school is sickness. So I guess you are sick." Stuart complained that he was not sick, but his mother stuck to her decision and put Stuart to bed. Still assuming he was sick, she did not allow him to play with his friends when they came home from school. He must have his rest.

The next morning Stuart was up, and out the door in time for the bus.

The consequence could have backfired easily if Mother had not maintained her resolve. If she had argued with Stuart about his being "sick" or lectured about being on time, the experience might not have been effective.

If the child is quite rebellious, and will fight about staying in bed, then a different approach may be needed.

Susie, age ten, had difficulty getting up in the morning. One morning she got up so late that she missed the bus. Mother decided that Susie, who had pulled this stunt many times before, was really "in school." About two o'clock her little brother Joey asked Mother if he could play with Susie's puzzles. Mother informed Joey that since Susie was not home he could not ask her permission until after school.

About a week later Susie again overslept. The same procedure followed. After a second time, however, Susie decided that getting up and going to school was better than staying home "alone."

Susie's mother refused to get involved in arguments with Susie about morning routine. She knew that Susie would soon become tired of staying home and learn to take the responsibility for getting herself to school. It took quite a bit of control to ignore Susie's presence for six hours. But if Susie had continually tried to involve her mother, she could have taken Joey and visited the neighbors or gone on short shopping trips.

After school

Al, age nine, and Shelly, age seven, rushed through the door, yelled "Hi, Mom," put their books down and proceeded to go out to play. Mother called, "Boys, come back here. You know you're supposed to change your clothes before going out to play." A few minutes later the boys were heard wrestling in their room. "I told you to change your clothes before playing—now get to it," their mother reprimanded angrily. She left, and the boys were quiet for a moment. Again she heard them wrestling. She rushed into their room and shook them. "Get those clothes changed!" Mother stood guard while the boys slowly changed their clothes.

About a half hour after the boys had gone out to play they came in for snacks, and then went outside again, leaving the kitchen a mess. Mother ran after them yelling, "You come back here this minute and clean up this mess!" The boys grudgingly returned to the kitchen to clean up. Mother had to check up on them three times before they finally finished cleaning.

As is the case when applying other principles of retraining, Mother must decide what she wants to accomplish. In this situation she may need to arrange a logical consequence to impress on the boys the value of changing their clothes after school. She can say to them, "I'm sorry, boys, if you're not responsible enough to change your clothes, then I guess you're not ready to go out. We'll try again tomorrow."

Mother can handle the messy kitchen situation by temporarily staging a "sitdown strike." This is a perfect opportunity for her to stand firm on her own convictions. When the boys come home in the evening asking, "When is dinner? What are we having?" Mother can reply, "I'm sorry, boys, but I don't cook in a messy kitchen." She has not told them what they must do, she has simply stated her intentions. If she remains friendly but firm and refuses to discuss it further, it won't take the boys long to figure out what to do about the untidy kitchen.

Alternatively Mother can clean the kitchen herself. Then, the next day when the boys come to the kitchen for a snack, she can say, "It appears that you are not quite ready to take the responsibility for cleaning up after snacks. So I'm afraid there'll be no snack today. We'll see what happens tomorrow."

Dinner time

Dinner time can be quite hectic in many families. Some children have to be called several times, others refuse to eat certain foods, brothers and sisters misbehave at the table.

One of the ways parents can learn more effective ways to relate to their children is through participating in parent study groups. A parent study group meets on a regular basis with a trained leader to discuss solutions to child-raising problems. (See Chapter 11 for further details about parent study groups.) At a weekly meeting of a parent study group, problems that occur at mealtime were discussed.

MRS. Y.: My two children are always busy playing when dinner is ready. Every night I have to drag them to the table. Both my husband and I are exasperated by the time we sit down to eat.

C. (counselor): What does the group think is happening in this situation?

MR. A.: It seems to me that the children are in a power contest with Mrs. Y. and her husband. The parents want to eat at a certain time, and the children want to eat when they feel like it.

C.: I agree. Does anyone have a suggestion as to what might be done?

MRS. D.: I had the same problem with my seven-year-old. I told him that I would call him to the table once. He could come or not come as he chose. If he came to the table while we were still eating, he was welcome to eat with us. If not, he could join us for breakfast in the morning. He missed dinner twice, and after that he came on time.

MR. M.: We tried that too, but it didn't work for us because our son would raid the refrigerator, and I ended up fighting with him about snacks.

C.: Has anyone else had that problem?

MRS. O.: I had it. My neighbor, who attended the group last term, suggested that I tell the children that snacks are for those who eat their supper. But my daughter would sneak the snacks. I finally had to lock them in a cabinet.

MR. M.: Isn't locking up things drastic? Shouldn't the children learn to stay out of cabinets without the aid of locks?

C.: I agree that it would be better if the children respected your decision in the matter. But the problem is that some of them do not. This is generally due to an ineffective relationship. In a good relationship we hear and respect each other. In order to build a good relationship we have to learn to avoid power struggles. Therefore, at this point it is much better to lock up snacks than to fight about them.

MRS. D.: How would you approach this with the children?

MRS. E.: I approached my daughter in the morning before she left for school because this is one of the calmer times in our house. I said, "It appears that you are not yet ready to accept the responsibility for leaving snacks alone. Therefore I will have to lock them up. Tomorrow I will take the locks off and see how it goes."

C.: I think it is important to emphasize the importance of timing. Mrs. E. approached her daughter at a time when she was feeling friendly toward her. Approaching a child at or near the time of conflict often heightens the conflict and turns a consequence into a punishment. Except for occasions when the child is causing a disturbance, or in a situation that requires immediate attention, it is best to choose a more relaxed time to discuss the problem.

MRS. R.: Should children who refuse to eat certain foods be required to eat a "no-thank-you portion"?

C.: Why do you think children refuse to eat certain foods?

MRS. O.: Probably because they don't like certain foods. All of us have our likes and dislikes.

C.: That's true, but how many of us have *grown* to like certain foods we didn't like in childhood?

MR. M.: I think I see what you mean. In other words, children sometimes use food as a weapon—to get parents involved in a power contest.

C.: That's my feeling. What do you think can be done about this?

MR. J.: Perhaps the family could discuss at their family

meeting certain foods that the members like and dislike and reach some sort of agreement.

MRS. D.: What do you mean?

MRS. J.: For instance, if the children did not like green beans, and the parents did, they could agree on how many nights to serve green beans. They could also decide how many nights to fix what the children like.

MRS. D.: That sounds like a great idea, but what if the children won't eat the green beans on the night they are served?

MRS. E.: Then the children can eat the other foods, as long as they do not deprive other members of their portions.

MRS. A.: What about children who eat very little of anything at the table?

MRS. O.: That is their right. They can eat again at breakfast. Here the "snacks are for those who eat their meals" would apply.

MRS. A.: Would the children be allowed their dessert if they didn't eat enough of the meal?

MR. J.: Is dessert part of the meal?

MRS. A.: Yes, I guess it is.

MR. J.: Then, in my opinion, it should be treated just like the other foods served. If we are going to let the children eat what they wish of what's offered, then they should be allowed the dessert too.

C.: I agree. Too often dessert is used to force children to eat other portions of the meal. I think we can gain more cooperation from our children if we don't use dessert as a weapon.

MR. J.: I am wondering about what to do with a child who is a *very* picky eater and just won't eat many different kinds of foods.

MRS. S.: We had that problem. My son dislikes many foods. In fact, he usually will eat very little of anything except fish. I discussed this with him, and I asked him if he would like to eat nothing but fish for a week. He jumped at the idea. I bought some of those frozen fish cakes, and for one week I served him fish for breakfast, lunch, and dinner. On the third day he was so tired of fish that he begged to eat what the rest of the family ate. I reminded him of our agreement. He was so sick of his favorite food by the end of the week that he was willing to eat anything placed before him.

C.: Although this consequence is quite strong, perhaps this one should be considered when all other approaches fail.

MRS. D.: My son and daughter are always arguing and fooling around at the table. We tell them to stop and sometimes send them to their rooms without supper, but they still carry on.

C.: Why do you suppose Mrs. D. is having difficulty?

MR. M.: It sounds as though her children might be making dinner time a battleground.

C.: What do you suppose they could do about it?

MRS. E.: Perhaps they should stop arguing and give the children the option of settling down or leaving the table. They could say something like, "Either settle down or leave the table—you decide."

MR. M.: Suppose they agreed to settle down and eat and then continued to fool around?

MRS. J.: Then you would know by their behavior what their real decision was and you could say, "I'm sorry, but I guess you decided to leave the table. Come back when you are ready to settle down."

MRS. D.: Suppose they don't go?

MRS. J.: Then you could ask them if they wished to leave of their own accord or if they would like you to help them. If they leave, no problem. If they don't, you just calmly lead them away.

MRS. D.: Suppose my children choose to leave the table and then come back in a few minutes and begin to fool around again. What should I do?

MR. J.: At that point you might say something like, "I'm sorry, but I see that you are still not ready. We will try again at breakfast." The next night they will remember how hungry they had been and they will probably settle down.

MR. M.: My son eats so slowly that we are forever waiting for him to finish. I tell him to hurry up and he does, but then he always slows down and I have to tell him again.

C.: What is the purpose of his son's behavior?

MRS. O.: It sounds as though his son has learned a very good way of gaining attention.

MRS. A.: Perhaps Mr. M. could inform his son that dinner will be over at a certain time. If he wishes to finish his meal, he will have to be done by that time. Then the dishes could be cleared whether or not he has finished. If he has not finished, he will not eat again until breakfast.

MR. M.: That sounds reasonable to me.

MRS. S.: My daughter has the opposite problem—she eats too fast.

C.: What do you do about it?

MRS. S.: I tell her to slow down, because it's not good for her stomach. Sometimes I tell her she can't leave until everyone's finished, but she continues to eat too fast.

C.: This is a difficult problem to solve. I think we can safely assume that Mrs. S. is involved in a power struggle with her daughter. Perhaps if Mrs. S. realized that there is really nothing she can do about the rate at which her daughter eats, she could stop worrying about it. When her daughter senses that Mother is no longer concerned about her eating problem, maybe she will slow down.

MRS. O.: Why would she slow down?

C.: Because it appears that she uses her speed of eating to engage her mother in battle. If Mrs. S. refuses to fight it, perhaps she will not eat as fast.

Bedtime

Bedtime presents a problem for many families. The parents want the children to go to bed so that they may have some time to themselves, and the children want to stay up, thinking that all kinds of magical things go on after they are in bed.

Jenny, nine, Greg, seven, and Neil, five, kept the house in an uproar at bedtime by getting up for drinks, making noises, and arguing. Out of desperation, their mother and father usually gave each child a spanking and then waited through the additional time the children spent crying until the house finally became quiet. This process began at 8:30 P.M. and ended approximately an hour later. In the morning all three children seemed to be rested despite the preceding night's battle.

These parents are in a losing battle with their children. First of all, many children do not need as much sleep as we think. If the child can function the next day on less sleep than the parent originally determines, then he has not made the best judgment of the child's requirements. It is generally advisable to establish separate and individual bedtimes related to the age of each child. The bedtimes can be negotiated with great benefit. The oldest child will receive the privilege of extended time, the negative interactions among the children will be eliminated, and the negotiations will provide an opportunity for the parent to communicate with each child individually and in a positive fashion.

If the parent cannot elicit cooperation by making agreements, then he may employ consequences. By being allowed to stay up as late as he pleases, the child will undoubtedly experience the natural consequences of not having enough sleep until he learns to go to bed at a reasonable hour.

INGREDIENTS FOR SUCCESS: PARENT RETRAINING

While natural and logical consequences provide a technique for raising the child, they cannot be truly successful unless the parent is flexible, courageous, and open to self-examination. Establishing a positive parent-child relationship requires the parent as well as the child to change. The following reviews some of the essential principles for parent retraining.

1. *Restrict talking to friendly conversation and use a respectful tone of voice:* To influence the child the parent must learn to curb his criticism and talk in a positive vein. His tone of voice should convey respect and value for his child as a person.

2. *Be both firm and kind:* When the parent decides upon a course of action, he must not vacillate, and he must remember to be friendly, nonjudgmental, and matter-of-fact when applying a consequence.

3. *Keep your control:* Children often try to gain control by demanding special attention. Responding with anger rarely accomplishes anything. The parent stands a much better chance of succeeding with his child by remaining calm, matter-of-fact, capable of planning an effective course of action.

4. *Utilize encouragement:* The parent can encourage the child by recognizing effort and contribution, as well as accomplishment, and by demonstrating that he understands how the child feels when things aren't going well. Unlike praise and reward, encouragement can be given even if the child is not entirely successful.

5. *Use natural and logical consequences:* A misbehaving child does not benefit from punishment. Instead, the parent must allow the child to experience reality's lessons through the use of logical and natural consequences.

6. *Have courage:* While the parent is retraining himself and his child, he may have to try out new methods several times. Changing behavior requires practice and patience. When new approaches fail, the parent should not despair, but stop and analyze his feelings and actions. Then he will learn how to proceed differently next time.

REFERENCES

Dreikurs, Rudolf, and Loren Grey. *A Parent's Guide to Child Discipline.* New York: Hawthorn Books, Inc., 1970, pp. 35–38.
————and Vicki Soltz. *Children: The Challenge.* New York: Duell, Sloan & Pearce, 1964.

CHAPTER 7

Consequences for Common Concerns

In addition to problems of daily routine, the principles of logical consequences are highly effective in dealing with a variety of behaviors and issues that parents are likely to encounter during the growth of their children.

FORGETFULNESS

Many parents find forgetfulness quite disturbing. They wonder why some children seem unable to remember anything. As with all behavior and misbehavior, forgetfulness is best understood by looking at its results.

> Susie seemed to forget everything. Each morning she would dash out to the bus only to have her mother call to remind her to take her school books and other materials.

Looking at the consequences of Susie's forgetting, the purpose becomes clear. Susie does not have to remember—her mother does it for her! Thus Susie has discovered an effective way of gaining her mother's attention and service. If Susie's mother would tell her that she is old enough to be responsible for remembering what to take to school, Susie would have to deal with the teacher, who would probably lend her books and materials only the first few times.

Eleven-year-old Barry had agreed to take out the trash each Tuesday and Thursday, but he would always forget. Mother would remind him before he left the house, but a few minutes later he had already forgotten again. Mother then began to watch to make sure he did not forget.

It appears that Barry does not want to keep his agreement. His forgetting is an attempt to try to avoid the task. If his mother is to cure Barry's forgetfulness, she must relinquish the responsibility of making sure he remembers. And since it is apparent that Barry does not wish to keep this agreement, she should discuss the problem with him in an effort to reach an alternative. She must hear Barry's feelings, send "I Messages," and work out a new agreement that is acceptable to both.

MOTHER: Barry, it seems to me that you really don't like the agreement we made concerning the trash.

BARRY: I don't.

MOTHER: I can understand how you feel. I guess it's a pretty unpleasant job. (Showing she can appreciate his feelings.)

BARRY: Those cans are heavy and dirty and smelly. I just hate that job!

MOTHER: It really makes you *very* angry? (Hearing feelings.)

BARRY: It sure does.

MOTHER: I can appreciate how you feel, but I have a problem too. I don't feel it's fair for me to have to do all the jobs in our house. How can we work this out? Is there some way both of us can be satisfied? (Seeking alternate solutions.)

BARRY: Maybe if you would take out the trash sometimes and I take it out sometimes, it wouldn't be so bad.

MOTHER: Okay, but I still feel that this would be putting an extra job on me, considering all the other things I have to do. ("I Message.")

BARRY: I could help with the dishes once in a while.

MOTHER: That sounds good to me. I'm really glad this problem is settled. That discussion was very helpful. ("I Message.")

Here Mother has made an attempt to deal with the problem in a constructive way. She approached Barry in a friendly manner and gave him a chance to express his feelings concerning the problem. She used reflective listening to show Barry she understands how he feels. She expressed her own feelings through "I Messages." Together they worked out a mutually agreeable solution. Mother has a good chance of winning cooperation. However, if Barry still persists in not keeping his agreements, Mother may have to utilize consequences or renegotiate to resolve the conflict. (See consequences for chores which appear later on in this chapter.)

When children habitually forget, parents must discover the purpose. Then they can select appropriate responses. In situations where the forgetting does not directly affect the parent, he should withdraw and let the natural consequences take place. In situations where the child's forgetting poses a problem for the parent, he should hear the child's feelings, express his own feelings, reach agreement, and then, if necessary, utilize consequences.

PETS

The care and feeding of pets presents a problem in some families. Parents have to keep after the children in order to see that the pet is taken care of. Obviously, the pet should not suffer because of neglect; therefore, logical consequences must be arranged in order to influence the children.

Nine-year-old Mark loved to play with his dog, but he often forgot to feed and give him water. Mother usually had to remind him several times. One evening, instead of prodding Mark, Mother decided to try a different approach. She said nothing to Mark and fed the dog herself. The next day Mark returned home from school and proceeded to look for his dog. He asked his mother where the dog was. Mother told him that she was sorry, but she had put the dog in the basement. Since Mark did not want to take care of the animal, then he did not have the right to play with it. If Mark decided to take care of the dog, he could then play with it. He promised that he would take care of his pet. Mother told him she would know by his behavior what he intended to do.

After supper Mark took food and water to the dog without being reminded. Mother then allowed him to play with his pet.

The next evening, however, Mark again forgot to feed his dog. Mother proceeded as before and fed the dog without comment. When Mark returned home from school the next day he again found the dog in the basement. Then he remembered that he had not fed his pet the previous evening. He asked Mother when he could play with the dog. Mother replied that he could try again the next day.

From then on Mark seldom avoided his responsibility of taking care of his pet. Whenever he did neglect the dog Mother simply placed the animal in the basement and denied Mark the right to play with his pet for a while.

Mother approached the problem in a matter-of-fact manner. She utilized Mark's desire to play with the animal in order to teach him responsibility concerning the care of the pet. "If you wish to play with the dog, you will have to be responsible for taking care of him." Each successive time Mark repeated his misbehavior she increased the amount of time Mark was denied the right to play with the animal. If at a later time Mark neglects the dog, she can begin the process over again.

Sometimes children do not wish to play with their pets as frequently as Mark did. In this case alternate approaches need to be utilized.

Mr. and Mrs. G. had four children, aged eight, ten, twelve, and fifteen. The family was having a problem with who was to feed the family dog. At a family meeting it was decided to share the feeding of the animal. All family members, including the parents, agreed to take turns caring for the pet. It was decided that a weekly rotation schedule would be set up.

The parents reported that their feeding problem was greatly decreased.

This family utilized the family meeting to mutually work out a solution to a common problem. The fact that *all* family members agreed to take turns explains the effectiveness of the procedure. When Mother and Father participate in an unrelished chore the children are usually more willing to cooperate.

In some families neither of the two preceding approaches are successful. In this instance the relationship between parents and children may be too strained to gain cooperation. At this point the parents can discuss with the children whether the animal is really worth the work involved. If they say yes, but continue to neglect him, the parents may have to give the animal away. This should be done only as a last resort, however, as it may be viewed with much resentment on the part of the children.

What should parents do when children abuse their pet?

> Five-year-old Jenny liked to hit Jake, the family's Schnauzer. Whenever Jenny did this Jake would snap at her, causing Jenny to scream. Mother would rush in, slap Jake, and then scold Jenny for bothering the dog. However, this action did not stop Jenny from pestering the dog.

Since Jenny repeated the misbehavior, it appears that although she obviously did not enjoy being snapped at or scolded, she did enjoy the attention she got from Mother.

In most cases a pet is a natural ally to parents who are teaching children the proper treatment of animals. Family dogs will not hurt the children and can be allowed to deal with mistreatment problems. (If the family has a pet they feel cannot be trusted, perhaps the family should reconsider the value of keeping such an animal.) If Mother had not interfered in this situation, Jenny would have learned not to bother Jake. As it was, Jenny was willing to be snapped at in order to get Mother involved.

In some situations where toddlers are involved, parents may wish to proceed differently to avoid possible accidental injury to the child.

> Eighteen-month-old Jimmy loved to hug and pet the family dog. One day he began to pull the dog's ear and the animal let out a yell. Even though the noise startled Jimmy, he pulled at the dog's ear again. Mother, who was standing by, picked up the boy and put him in his room and closed the door. A few minutes later Mother let Jimmy out of the room. He began to play with the dog again, and again pulled his ear. Mother picked up Jimmy again and put him in his room and left him there about twice as long as before. After she let him out of the room Jimmy went to play with the dog, but this time he did not pull his ear.

Children as young as Jimmy do not comprehend a verbal choice. By her action Mother has taught Jimmy that he may play with the dog as long as he does not mistreat him.

KITCHEN CHORES

> Pat, ten, had agreed at a family meeting to set the table each evening. For the next few days the agreement was kept. Toward the end of the week, however, Pat began to "forget" her commitment. Mother had to remind and coax her.

It appears that Pat is not yet willing to keep her agreement. Mother is kept busy reminding and coaxing. The responsibility for the chore at this point belongs to Mother. If Mother wishes to help Pat assume responsibility, she will need to stop talking and act. She will have to utilize logical consequences to help Pat see the effects of irresponsibility.

Instead of reminding and coaxing, Mother should state her intentions. When she notices that the table has not been set, she should leave the kitchen and occupy herself with other pursuits. When Pat asks about dinner she could say, "I can't serve dinner because the table isn't set."

While it may seem unfair for the rest of the family to wait for their dinner, if mother begins reminding and coaxing, Pat will not learn to assume responsibility. A responsible person normally does what needs to be done. If the family is to be a unit, each member making his contribution for the good of all, then there has to be some interdependence. However, in cases where a problem of irresponsibility persists, stronger action may be needed.

Mr. and Mrs. L. had four children: Don, ten, Gary, nine, Jane, seven, and Joyce, two. At a family meeting the three older children had agreed to work together in clearing the table after dinner and doing the dishes. They had also agreed that any time they used the kitchen to make themselves a snack after school, the kitchen would be put in order. After a few days the novelty wore off and the children began to "forget" to fulfill their agreements.

One evening after supper the children ran off to play, completely ignoring their job of clearing the table. The next morning Mrs. L. stayed away from the kitchen; however, since the children enjoyed fixing their own breakfast, this had no effect on the kitchen-mess situation. After snack time was over that day, there wasn't a clean dish left in the kitchen.

As dinner time approached, the children began to ask Mrs. L. when they would eat. She replied, "I'm sorry, children, but I can't cook in a messy kitchen." The children began to argue among themselves as to whose job it was to clean up, but no one made a move to actually do it.

When Mr. L. returned home from work the kitchen was still a mess. Mr. L. took one look and went into the family room, saying to Mrs. L., "Come on, honey, we're going out for dinner." The children said, "Super! Where are we going, Dad?" Mr. L. replied, "Oh, I didn't mean you older children—just Mother, Joyce, and I are going." The children said, "But we haven't had any supper yet." Dad replied,

"Well, I guess you'll have to take care of that yourselves."

When Mr. and Mrs. L. returned home the kitchen had been cleaned up and the children had fixed supper for themselves.

Mr. and Mrs. L. handled the problem effectively. The two-year-old was too young to be left to experience the consequences created by the older children. Mrs. L. has a right to state under what conditions she will prepare meals. She is doing the cooking, so if she does not wish to cook in a messy kitchen, she can refuse to prepare dinner when the kitchen has not been cleaned.

The approach is also useful when a child breaks an agreement to empty the kitchen wastebasket. If the trash begins to pile up, Mother can state her intentions: "I'm sorry, but I don't like to work in a kitchen where there is a lot of garbage." If this simple statement does not get the job done, the parents may need to take action similar to Mr. and Mrs. L.'s.

When a parent states an intention, the statement must always be backed up with action in order to be effective. You need only state your intentions once. Repeated statements lose their effect—action is much more effective.

TRASH CANS AND WASTEBASKETS

Unpleasant chores, such as emptying wastebaskets and garbage cans, present a problem in many families. It seems that parents almost universally give these jobs to the children. Why? Such menial, undesired tasks have been traditionally allocated to those who are considered of lower status. Parents who consider their children to be inferior human beings, as many parents do, naturally give these types of jobs to children. While the child may resent being the "family trash collector," at beginning family meetings, when given a chance to choose the chores he is willing to do, he may choose those his parents had previously assigned to him.

If these jobs aren't completed, the parents will have to take some action. With the exception of unemptied kitchen garbage cans, in which case Mother can refuse to work in a kitchen where there is a lot of garbage, there is no directly related consequence. One family solved the problem thus:

> Mr. and Mrs. T's son, Mike, had agreed to empty the garbage cans. Mike often forgot to do his job, but when given an opportunity to change jobs, he declined. Mr. T. asked Mike what he thought should be done if he forgot to do his job. Mike replied that he did not know. Mr. T. explained that when he wanted to get his car washed, but did not want to do it himself, he had to pay someone to do his job. He then said that if Mike forgot, he would be willing to take out the trash for him, since it had to be done. But since it was not his job, he would expect Mike to pay him for it. Mike agreed, and a price was negotiated. For the first two weeks Mike let Dad assume the job. After Mike received the "bill" for the second week, however, he decided he would do his job himself and keep the money instead of paying his father.

Mr. T. approached this problem in a logical fashion. Mike was not forced to take out the cans. He was given the opportunity to change jobs, which he did not do. Mr. T. explained paying for service in a way that made sense to Mike. Mike agreed and had the opportunity to choose whether or not to do the chore. This approach could be adaptable to other chores as long as it is not over done. Using money in too many instances will often create rebellion, bargaining, and a power struggle.

CHILDREN'S ROOMS

One of the most difficult problems to solve is the care of children's bedrooms. Parents are constantly reminding children to keep their rooms in order. When parents have an ineffective relationship with their child, he often becomes uncooperative in areas that are most important to his parents. Neatness often becomes one such issue with parents who find it very difficult to tolerate messy rooms.

As with hair styles and taste in clothing, many children feel that they have a right to keep their rooms as they wish. They consider their bedrooms to be their personal domains. Parents stand a better chance of influencing their children toward orderliness if they respect the children's wishes in the matter. Creating battlegrounds over rooms seldom teaches children to be neat. They continue being messy in order to show parents that they cannot be forced to be neat. Parents must withdraw from such a power contest.

Parents should acknowledge the child's right to keep his own room the way he wishes. The bedroom door can be closed if the mess bothers the parents. Without the parents' distress over the room's condition, the child can gain no payoff for his misbehavior and often becomes tired of the mess himself. This usually takes quite a long time, however.

But parents have rights too. Mother has the right not to enter the child's room to change his sheets if she does not like the mess. She can tell the child that she is not willing to enter a room that is messy, and offer to help him clean the room once a week on a mutually agreed-on time. Often children will respond to this offer of help if Mother is not insistent that they accept her offer. If the child does not wish to clean up his room, or does not really participate in the effort, Mother can leave the clean sheets outside the room for the child to take care of. If he does not change the sheets after a reasonable time, Mother can assume that he does not want them, and put away the clean sheets. She should make her offer of help and clean sheets, and if the child does not respond, she should not bring the subject up again unless the child asks. Both parents can refuse to enter the room for any purpose.

In cases where Mother has agreed at a family meeting to clean the child's room if it is "in order," she can refuse to clean the room if the child has not straightened it up.

Mother can also refuse to allow the child to invite his friends to play in his room if it is not clean. The child should not be restricted from playing with his friends, but he will have to play somewhere else than in his room.

There are times when children's rooms must be kept in fairly neat order—for example, when out-of-town guests are visiting for a few days or when the family is trying to sell their house. If this is the situation, alternate approaches may need to be utilized.

Mr. and Mrs. P. were trying to sell their house. Mrs. P. felt that the entire house should be in reasonable order for prospective buyers to view. Ten-year-old Kathy did not like to keep her room neat. Mrs. P. explained to Kathy that she realized that Kathy had a right to keep her room as she wished, but that since the family was trying to sell the house, all rooms would need to be kept neat in order to make a favorable impression on prospective buyers. Mrs. P. asked Kathy if she would keep her room reasonably neat until the house was sold. Kathy promised that she would.

For a week Kathy did an adequate job, but then she began to let the room go. One evening Mother approached her. "I'm going to clean the house tomorrow, and if your room is not straightened up, I will have to clean it myself. I don't feel it's fair for me to have to take time to put everything away, so I'll put the articles I find lying around into paper bags and place them in the basement."

Kathy made no reply and did not take care of her room. Mother followed through with what she had said. Kathy had difficulty locating some of her things and had to look through the bags. For a day or two she kept her room neat. Then she began to let the room get messy again. This time Mother said nothing, but she put into paper bags whatever she found out of place. As Kathy began to miss more of her belongings she began to keep the room more orderly. When she would occasionally "forget," Mother would get out the paper bags.

Mother was in a difficult position. She could not let the room go; she had to keep the house in reasonable condition each day. She appealed for Kathy's help and received it for a while. When Kathy began to become irresponsible, Mother had no other choice but to take some kind of action. Mother acted wisely by not fighting with Kathy over the cleaning of the room. She simply did what was needed in order to clean the room, but at the same time did not inconvenience herself any more than was necessary. If Mother would have put things away for Kathy, there would have been no reason for Kathy to assume the responsibility of her room. Kathy became tired of rummaging through the bags and decided to put things away.

An alternate approach to the paper bags would be to negotiate a fee for straightening the child's room such as was mentioned in the example of the garbage cans. This can also be an effective approach for the parent who "screams with his mouth closed" or lets it be plainly observed that he is bothered by the messy room.

In situations such as described the children understood the logic of the consequences. In everyday situations, however, children may view these same consequences as attempts to force them to clean their rooms. As with all child-training procedures, the method must fit both the child and the parent.

These techniques can also be appropriate when the parent feels that the over-all relationship has improved, but the room is still a problem.

TELEVISION

Television is often blamed for many parental difficulties. It interferes with the children's chores, homework, and bedtime, they contend. Interestingly enough, however, when the parents turn off the television set they often still experience much difficulty in getting the jobs done. Many children use television to evade, put off, or "forget" what they are supposed to do. By doing so they are sending the parents a message: "I don't intend to do what you want me to if I can help it." Therefore, when parents find that television is interfering with their children's responsibilities, it is time to examine the relationship.

Some parents create battlegrounds over television by arbitrarily restricting its use. This approach often causes resentment and retaliation on the part of the children. Also, parents are often inconsiderate of children's wishes in regard to favorite programs. Many parents would resent their child's interference when they are watching a favorite movie on the set. Yet these same parents think nothing of demanding that a certain chore or task be done immediately, whether or not the child is watching a program.

If parents wish to gain the children's cooperation regarding the use of television, as in any other area of conflict, they must take the children's interests and preferences into consideration. This can be an opportunity to share feelings and values and reach mutually agreed-on decisions.

Some children occupy most of their time in watching television. These children may be using television to escape reality. They prefer and feel safer in the fantasy world of television. In this case, parents should discuss with the child the amount of time he spends in watching television and come to an agreement about how much time each day can be spent this way. Then the child may select the programs he wishes to watch during his "TV time."

The television set often presents an excellent opportunity for the children to learn to share.

> Mrs. L. had three children, ages nine, eleven, and twelve. Typically, the three children would argue over what program to watch. Mrs. L. would usually warn them that unless they stopped arguing she would turn off the set and they would have to go to their rooms. The children would settle for a while, then start again. After about three warnings Mrs. L. would carry through with her threat. Although this method resolved the problem for the moment, later in the day, or the next day, the children would begin again.
>
> One day when the children were arguing, Mrs. L. decided

to make out a schedule of what they should watch. "Joyce, you may watch what you want until four o'clock. Then, Jimmy, you may watch what you want until four-thirty. And, Sam, you may watch what you want until five." No sooner had Mother announced her decision than the children began to complain that they did not like the way the schedule was made out. Mrs. L. then became quite frustrated and said, "Okay, if you don't like the schedule I've made out, then none of you can watch television. Make up your minds!" The three children grumbled and agreed to follow the schedule. No sooner had Mother returned to the kitchen than the two boys began to tease Joyce and try to keep her from watching her program. Mrs. L. then went into the family room and sent all three children to their rooms.

It looked as though Mrs. L.'s children had discovered a clever way to defeat Mother at every turn. If she was going to clear up this situation, she had to refuse to fight about the use of the television, stop trying to solve the problem for the children, and treat the situation in a different way.

The next time the children began to argue about the television, Mrs. L. very calmly went into the family room, turned off the set, and said to her children, "Whenever you three decide on what program to watch, let me know and I'll turn the set back on." Mrs. L. left the room. In a few minutes one of the children came to inform her that they had reached a decision. Mrs. L. then turned the set on again.

Mrs. L. found that this procedure reduced the arguing in the future.

Mrs. L. has placed the responsibility for using the television where it belongs—with the children. By refraining from becoming angry, warning, punishing, and trying to "make" them share, she has refused to reinforce their attempts to overpower her. She simply stated the condition of television-watching *once*, and showed by her action what she intended to do.

To further reduce the daily quarreling, Mr. and Mrs. L. could have the children develop a schedule at the family meetings. This approach is more desirable than making a schedule for them, as it involves the children themselves in the scheduling. The subject can be introduced by asking the children what they think they can do to avoid future difficulties. Hopefully, they will come up with the idea of making a viewing schedule that will be satisfactory to all three children. If they do not come up with the idea, it may be suggested in order to see what the children think. If they agree that it would be a good idea, then Mother and Father can help them work it out. If not, then the idea will have to be dropped.

Forcing the children to make a schedule and adhere to it usually produces only more uncooperative behavior. If there are no arguments, then a schedule is not necessary after all. If, however, the arguments continue, the television set can be turned off until the next meeting. Mother can say, "It seems that you are not yet ready to share the television, therefore I will have to turn it off, and we can discuss the problem at our next meeting." By the next meeting the children should be ready to seriously discuss the issue.

If they make a schedule, but indicate by quarreling that they are not willing to follow their agreement, the set should be turned off until the next family meeting.

Some children will attempt to defeat parents when this approach is used by turning the set back on. This action is an invitation to fight. In this case the parent needs to remain calm, go about his business, and at a later time remove a tube from the set. Then at the next family meeting the problem can be discussed.

At times parents will restrict television viewing as a punishment in order to force the children to do what is expected of them. Children who bring home poor report cards or refuse to do their chores are often denied the privilege of watching television. This approach is usually ineffective, as is any retaliatory act, and often invites further misbehavior.

CARE OF PERSONAL BELONGINGS

"Scott and Janet, you come here this minute!" shouted Mother. "Now, pick up these toys. Why do I always have to tell you to pick up after yourselves?"

This scene is not uncommon. Parents often complain that their children strew their possessions about the house, leaving them with the unpleasant choice between having to keep after the children to pick things up or do the chore themselves. What these parents don't realize is that they can approach the problem in a variety of effective ways.

> Mrs. B. had three children—Mike, eleven, Joan, ten, and Sharon, five. The children would often neglect to put their belongings away.
> At the supper table Mrs. B. said to her children, "I find your things scattered around the house. I don't like to see the house messy, so from now on I'll put the things I find into a box in the garage. If you are missing anything, you can look in the box."

Mrs. B. approached the problem in a friendly spirit. She did not lecture and preach to the children about how they should pick up things. She used an "I Message" to convey to them how she feels about the situation, and stated her intentions. It was up to the children to decide if they wished to put their belongings away or search through the box. In most cases children become tired of rummaging through a box every time they want something they have carelessly left lying around, and they begin to pick up after themselves. Parents have to be reminded that, considering the number of possessions children have today, this consequence may take time to be effective.

If it appears that the children are indifferent and still do not put their things away, the parent may want to use the "mystery box" technique. The parent can inform the children that why they still leave things out of place has been a mystery, but that he can no longer be their slave. In the future when something must be picked up, the parent will place it in a box that will not be available to the children, and it will also be a mystery as to when the item will be returned. The object can then be returned to its proper storage place after any length of time that appears to be effective in teaching the consequence.

A third way of approaching the problem is to put the objects away. When the children ask for something, they are told that it appears that they have not yet learned to put things away, and so they may not have the object, but they may try again the next day. After the allotted time the child is given back the article. If he continues to leave things out of place, then his belongings will be removed for two days, and so on.

Some parents tell their children they will throw out everything they find lying around. This approach is usually ineffective because it is interpreted by the children as revenge and invites similar retaliation.

PERSONAL HYGIENE

Clothing and grooming

Many parents today are greatly concerned about the clothing and hair styles of their children, especially those who are teen-agers. Each generation of preteen and teen-age children in the past several decades has had its own particular style of appearance, perpetuated by peer acceptance rather than adult approval. Parents tend to create battlegrounds over fads, forgetting that the clothes they wore as youngsters once aggravated their own parents.

Joy, age eleven, and her mother often argued intensely over what Joy was to wear to school. Mother complained that she did not approve of her daughter's choice of clothing, while Joy bitterly responded that all her friends dressed in this particular fashion and that she would be a social outcast if she wasn't allowed to dress accordingly. Mother said that she was not concerned with what Joy's friends wore. "No daughter of mine is going to look like a tramp!" Mother usually succeeded in making Joy wear what she considered proper. But each argument ended in intense negative feelings between mother and daughter.

Mother may win the battle over what Joy wears, but she may also lose her relationship with her daughter. Creating battlegrounds over minor issues often hampers parental influence in major situations. Why was Mother so concerned about how Joy dressed for school? It appears that she felt that Joy's appearance was a reflection on herself as a mother. Thus her concern for her own prestige impairs her relationship with her daughter. In actuality, Joy's dress should be regarded as an expression of herself and her own tastes; in no way does it reflect upon her mother.

It is our feeling that children as well as adults have a right to dress and groom themselves as they see fit. Of course there are some exceptions to this in terms of school and business regulations. But many schools are no longer establishing dress and grooming codes, a move that will faciliate learning by eliminating one of the battlegrounds between the school and its students.

Another exception to freedom of dress is the family outing.

Nine-year-old David seemed to hate to wear anything that did not contain at least one large area of dirt. Mother and Father constantly argued with David about what he was to wear when the family went out. He often made the family late. After discussing the problem at a parent group meeting, the parents decided to try a new approach.

The next evening, when the family was going out for dinner, David came out of his room dressed in his usual spotted attire, waiting for the conflict to begin. Father said, "I'm sorry, Dave, but we are not willing to take you with us in those clothes. If you would like to join us for dinner, you will need to wear your clean dress-up clothes." David complained that he did not like his dress-up clothes and that he did not intend to change. Father replied, "Okay, Julie will be up to sit in a few minutes, and we'll see you when we get home." David rushed back to his room and quickly changed his clothes.

Parents have a right to say what attire they are willing to accept when they are taking the children out. Father succeeded in his attempt on this particular evening without the usual exhausting battle because he simply stated what he was willing to accept, gave Dave a choice, and planned in advance in case his son decided not to change his clothes. It is obvious from the result that Dave did not wish to be left out of family activities, but was in a power contest with his parents. When Father refused to fight and provided Dave with an alternative, Dave's attempt to show his power was futile.

Cleanliness

Brushing teeth, washing hands, and taking baths create problems for many families. Logical consequences need to be arranged in order to impress upon the children the necessity of keeping clean.

Frank, age six, would not brush his teeth in the morning before school. Mother discussed the problem with a friend, who reported that she had solved the same problem by telling her children that since sweets cause tooth decay, she would have to discontinue providing sweets if they were not willing to brush their teeth.

Frank's mother decided to give this a try. One evening before bedtime Mother told Frank about sweets, tooth decay, and brushing. The next morning, however, Frank did not brush his teeth. That afternoon, after school, Frank asked for a snack. Mother told him that he could have an apple or an orange. "Why can't I have some cookies?" asked Frank. "I'm sorry, but you didn't brush your teeth this morning," was his mother's reply. Frank grudgingly accepted an apple.

For the next few days Frank remembered to brush his teeth. Then he began to "forget" again. When he came home from school he would ask for his treat. Mother would offer him some fruit. "Why can't I have some cookies? I brushed my teeth this morning." Mother knew that he had not. She did not answer, handed Frank an apple, and left the room.

This pattern was repeated often.

One day Mother said to her son, "Frank, suppose you hang a pencil on a string by the calendar, and every morning after you brush your teeth, you can make an X on the date. When you come home from school you can check to see if you have brushed your teeth, and then you will know what kind of snack you may have. That way you can keep track of yourself." Frank agreed to this.

Mother reported that Frank would check his calendar each afternoon and choose his snack accordingly.

Frank's mother has used a logical approach to a common problem. Frank can brush or not brush as he chooses, and his mother will follow through with action instead of talk. In addition, Mother has developed a way to place the responsibility for checking up with Frank, an action that indicates her trust in her son. Without Mother checking up on him, Frank's lies will not provoke an argument; thus his desire to lie is diminished. Eventually Frank will no longer need the calendar marking, and his mother can suggest that it be discontinued.

Jimmy, age ten, seemed to accumulate more than his share of dirt on his hands. Each night before supper Mother would tell him to wash. He would return to the table having barely run the water over his hands, and his mother would send him back with chastising remarks. It took at least three round trips before Mother would accept him at the table. By this time the entire family was angry with Jimmy's lack of cooperation.

Jimmy manages to keep the family in an uproar and make dinner time unpleasant by his misbehavior. Mother unknowingly contributes to the problem by sending him back several times and by chastising him. Mother can retrain Jimmy, win his cooperation, and help make the dinner hour more enjoyable by changing her approach.

Jimmy comes to the table with dirty hands. Mother removes his plate and says, "I'm sorry, but I'm not willing to serve someone with dirty hands."

Jimmy leaves the dining room, but returns in a few minutes having barely washed his hands. "Okay, my hands are clean, can I sit down now?" Mother does not answer, but continues her conversation with Dad. Jimmy stands by the table for a few seconds, then takes his seat and says, "Well, can I have my plate now?" Mother still does not answer. In a few seconds Jimmy goes to the bathroom. When he returns, it is clear that he has really washed his hands. Mother places his plate on the table.

Mother has remained firm but kind, stating her intentions concerning serving someone with dirty hands, and then acting accordingly. When Jimmy returned the first time after "going through the motions" of hand-washing, Mother refrained from further comment and showed Jimmy by her actions that she did not consider his hands clean. He understood and decided to wash them in order to get his dinner. In the future if Jimmy comes to the table with dirty hands, Mother should make no remarks but simply remove his plate. Jimmy will know what to do.

If Jimmy had had to make several trips to the bathroom before his hands were clean, and if he had wasted so much time that dinner was over by the time he decided to get the job done, then he would have had to miss his meal.

Getting children to take baths is another trouble spot in many homes. Parents can influence their children without conflict by creating logical consequences that will impress the children with the necessity of taking baths. If the family is going out for an evening, they can refuse to take the children unless they are clean. But family outings do not usually occur as often as baths are needed. One father solved the bath problem like this.

Jan, age seven, had a distaste for bathing and would go for several days without a bath. One night while the family was watching television, Father said, "I'm sorry, Jan, but you have an odor. If you wish to stay here with us, you will have to bathe." Jan grudgingly left the family room, bathed, and rejoined the family.

This approach is risky, as the child may view it as insulting. However, Jan's father did offer her a choice. He did not order her to bathe, but rather told her that if she wished to remain with them she would have to bathe.

An alternate approach to the bathing problem is to prohibit putting clean clothes on a dirty body.

Kevin, age nine, would seldom bathe without constant nagging from Mother. One morning when Kevin was getting ready for school, Mother said, "I'm sorry, Kevin, but you can't put clean clothes on a dirty body. You'll have to wear dirty clothes." Kevin decided to bathe.

If Kevin had decided to wear the dirty clothes, Mother should have respected his right to choose the alternative. If he continued to choose not to bathe and wear dirty clothes, his peers would most likely begin to let him know how they felt about his appearance and odor. He would probably then have decided to bathe.

Carelessness

Jenny, age nine, was very careless. One wintry day she lost her gloves at school. Her mother was very angry and lectured Jenny on the value of the gloves and the necessity to make sure that they were firmly tucked into her coat pocket. Then she called the school and inquired if anyone had found the gloves. Finally, since Mother did not want Jenny to have cold hands, she bought her daughter another pair of gloves.

Jenny has her mother in her control. As long as she is willing to put up with Mother's scolding, she does not have to assume the responsibility of looking after her possessions. For no matter what happens, even an angry mother will take care of the problem.

Mother must learn to place the responsibility for Jenny's belongings on Jenny's shoulders. Next time she might handle the situation this way:

MOTHER: I'm sorry you lost your gloves, Jenny.

JENNY: What am I going to do?

MOTHER: I don't know, but I'm sure you'll figure something out.

JENNY: Will you buy me another pair?

MOTHER: I'm sorry, but I don't feel I should spend more money on gloves. If you wish to spend your allowance money, I'll be glad to take you to the store with me the next time I go.

In this example, Mother helps Jenny realize that she must be responsible for her own possessions. She refuses to become angry and assume ownership of the problem while at the same time she offers Jenny a choice of buying new gloves with her own money or going without. Jenny must make the decision. The consequences of her carelessness will undoubtedly influence her behavior more than Mother's anger and instant solutions of the past.

When children lose or break things, parents should utilize consequences appropriate to the situation. For example, if the child loses or breaks one of his own possessions, he may replace it with his own money or go without—it is his problem. It is not the parents' problem if the child breaks or loses something that belongs to a sibling; it is a problem to be resolved between the children. If the broken or lost object belongs to the parents, the child would be required to make restitution.

BEHAVIOR IN THE FAMILY CAR

It is impossible to tell how many families have experienced close calls or serious accidents because they didn't know how to deal with disturbing behavior while driving. There are some

alternatives to common procedures. At the first sign of misbehavior the parent can pull to the side of the road and inform
the children in a kind but firm manner that he will continue
driving as soon as they settle down. If, after resuming the trip,
the misbehavior is repeated, the parent should pull over and
stop without comment until the disturbance stops. It should
not take too many pauses before the children will tire of their
game.

There are times, in local jaunts about the city—shopping
trips, and so on—where Mother cannot provide a sitter and
has to take the children with her when they do not want to go.
Cooperation of children who are dragged along against their
will is often very difficult to achieve. Effective procedures are
available, however. The parent can arrange her trips so that she
can do her errand and return in time for the children to watch
a favorite TV program or engage in some other enjoyable activity. At the first sign of disturbance Mother can pull over and
say something such as, "Your cartoon show begins at four
o'clock. If we're going to get back home in time for your show,
we have just enough time to drive to the store, shop, and drive
home." If the children repeat the disturbance, Mother can
stop again. If the children miss their activity and complain,
Mother should ignore the complaints.

RELATIONSHIPS WITH FRIENDS, NEIGHBORS, AND RELATIVES

When parents have a problematic relationship with their children, the children often display uncooperative behavior in situations where the parents are most vulnerable, such as in the
presence of friends, neighbors, or relatives.

Many parents who apply our methods with their children
when they are at home tend to discard them and return to ineffective means when others are present. When questioned as
to why they do this, replies such as "Jim's mother would not

understand the new ways" or "What would my neighbor think?" are often heard. We often ask such parents which they consider more important, impressing others or their relationship with their children.

> Bobby, age six, had a fight with a neighborhood boy in the churchyard after services. He ran to his father crying. Realizing the purpose of his act, his father decided to ignore his bid for attention and pity. "I know that hurts, Bobby," he said, and made no further comment. Another father standing near the scene inquired why Bobby's father did not attend to the matter as the boy seemed hurt. Before Father could reply, Bobby's mother comforted Bobby's hurt feelings by drawing him close and telling him everything would be all right. She was quite upset with Father's actions.
> Later she admitted that she probably would not have been as concerned if others had not been on the scene.

The real reason for Bobby's mother's concern was her imagined loss of status in the eyes of the bystanders. Bobby's father, on the other hand, showed Bobby that he understood how he felt, but he refused to become involved. He realized that overplaying such a situation might pave the way for similar misbehavior in the future. Had Mother not interfered, Bobby would have learned that fighting does not win sympathy and special attention.

Some parents do not revert to old ineffective ways, but instead, try to make sure that their children are treated considerately by friends and relatives. In other words, they tell them how they wish to have their children treated. This is just as serious as being concerned about the opinions of others, and nothing can lose a friend or alienate a relative more quickly. If another adult deals with the child in a manner with which his parents do not agree, it is much better for the child and for his parents' relationship with the other person to allow him to deal with the child as he sees fit. Children are not helpless, they know how to deal with adults—usually much better than the adults know how to deal with them!

There are some exceptions to this of course. If a friend or relative who visits often deals with the child in a manner that displeases his parents, they can ask for cooperation, or, if this fails, make their contacts less frequent and of shorter duration, or visit the person without the child.

Mr. and Mrs. J. were trying to train their children to eat in an orderly way at the dinner table. Mrs. J.'s father would come for dinner two or three times a week, and he would render all their training useless. Grandfather did not believe in their new-fangled ways. He would cooperate with the children in their antics, and actually seemed to enjoy them. Through it all he ignored the pleas of the parents.

The parents found that Grandfather's visits became increasingly unpleasant and dreaded. The children were wild after Grandfather left. They decided to approach Grandfather directly.

Mr. and Mrs. J. explained to Grandfather that he was welcome in their home as long as he was willing to help them with their dilemma. Otherwise, perhaps it would be better if he stayed away for a while. Then they informed the children that their misbehavior would keep Grandfather from wanting to visit. If they wished him to come, they would have to behave in an acceptable manner.

Grandfather agreed to cooperate with them in their efforts, and he kept his word. Dinner times became much more pleasant.

Mr. and Mrs. J. handled the problem very effectively. Since they were in circumstances where Grandfather's frequent visits were destroying their efforts, it was their right to decide whether they wished this kind of situation to continue. While having been honest with Grandfather may have appeared cruel, mutual respect demands sharing honest feelings. This openness improves the parents' relationship with Grandfather, in contrast to the destructiveness that would result from harboring smoldering resentment.

Sometimes parents find themselves confronted with an irate

neighbor, when actually the problem is between the neighbor and their child. For example:

> NEIGHBOR: Mr. S., my wife told me that when your son Ronnie was here this afternoon, he broke one of our windows with a rock. My wife and I would like to know what you intend to do about this.

Mr. S. has been placed in a difficult situation. If he accepts the responsibility for his son's misbehavior, he may please the neighbor, but he will deny his son the opportunity to learn to be responsible for his own actions. If Mr. S. is overly concerned about his neighbor's impression of him as a parent, then he will probably punish his son and pay for the window. If he is more interested in his relationship with his son and in training Ronnie to be responsible, then he will handle the situation differently:

> MR. S.: I'm very sorry that this has happened, and I appreciate your letting me know. We're trying to help Ronnie learn to be responsible for his actions, and you could be very helpful in this matter if you would deal with him and handle the situation in any way you see fit. But I do believe he should be financially responsible for the window.

If the neighbor is cooperative, fine. If, on the other hand, the neighbor becomes annoyed and demands that Mr. S. take care of the matter, Mr. S. will have to guarantee that the window will be paid for. "All right, if you will tell me the cost of repairing the window, I will see that Ronnie pays you." Mr. S. should then work out arrangements with Ronnie about paying for the window. Possibly Mr. S. will pay the neighbor himself and then have Ronnie reimburse him. In this way Mr. S. will not antagonize the neighbor and will still leave the responsibility for paying for the damage with Ronnie.

> Nine-year-old Jay was the terror of the neighborhood. Mr. and Mrs. P. would get many phone calls from neighbors complaining that Jay had bullied their children. Father would lecture Jay, and spank him, all to no avail. There seemed to

be no way to keep him from picking on the neighbors' children. Jay appeared to want the reputation of bully or monster.

It is unfortunate that Jay feels he must bully others in order to secure a place in the neighborhood social strata. It is far more unfortunate that Jay's father contributes to Jay's discouragement by attempting to force him to stop bullying. When Mr. P. punishes his son, Jay finds even more reason to bully others, in order to get even.

What should Jay's parents do? When neighbors call about Jay's behavior, his parents should sympathize with the fact that the neighbor's child was hurt and say that they will handle the situation and do their utmost to see that it will not happen again in the future. Then the parents must approach Jay.

FATHER (calmly): Jay, it appears that you have not yet learned how to get along with others, so tomorrow you will have to stay in the house. You may try again the next day. (Logical consequence.)

JAY: They always call me names.

FATHER: You seem pretty angry about this. Why do you suppose they call you names? (Reflective listening and initiating exploration of alternatives.)

JAY: I don't know.

FATHER: What do you do when they call you names?

JAY: I hit them.

FATHER: And what do they do?

JAY: They tell their parents and get me in trouble.

FATHER: It seems to me that they like to get you angry and in trouble. (Proposing a tentative hypothesis.)

JAY: Yes, I guess so.

FATHER: What do you think you could do the next time they try? (Facilitating problem-solving.)

JAY: I don't know.

FATHER: Why don't we think about it? What might be a way to avoid being mad? (Facilitating problem-solving.)

JAY: I guess I could walk away.

FATHER: You're thinking that if you walk away they can't tease you. (Reflective listening.)

JAY: Yes.

FATHER: You know, Jay, I think you've got something there. But I'm wondering if you think they might try harder to get you mad the first few times you walk away? (Helping child become aware of possible resistance.)

JAY: Probably.

FATHER: Would you be willing to walk away the next time they tease you, to see what happens?

JAY: Yes, I guess so.

FATHER: Okay, let's see how it goes.

Father's handling of the situation was far more beneficial to Jay than lecturing and punishing. He applied a logical consequence in order to improve the situation in the neighborhood and to help Jay understand that he must learn to manage his behavior if he wished to play with others. He also recognized Jay's feelings and helped Jay understand his problem and seek an alternate solution to fighting. Finally he got a commitment from Jay on future behavior. If Jay does not keep his promise, he may have to stay home for two days the next time he misbehaves.

Parents often dread the visit of particular neighborhood children whom their children have chosen as playmates. Often they are faced with the misbehavior of a neighbor's child in their own home. For example:

Mrs. T.'s son, Darren, age seven, had struck up a friendship with Brad, a son of a neighbor down the street. Brad was an only child, quite spoiled and pampered by his parents. He was undisciplined and seemed to feel he was entitled to do as he pleased.

After one of Brad's visits Mrs. T. noticed that her pen was missing. Darren said he did not know what had happened to it. When Mrs. T. asked him if he and Brad had been playing in the den, Darren shook his head and then added that he had sent Brad into the den to get some glue for a model they were building. Mother then asked Darren if he thought that Brad might have taken the pen. He replied that he did not know.

After a thorough search of the house Mrs. T. decided to ask Brad if he had seen the pen. The next day Brad came to play with Darren. "Brad, when you were here yesterday, did you see my pen?" Brad replied "No," his face red. Mrs. T. surmised from his self-consciousness that Brad had taken the pen. She then said, "I'm sorry, Brad, but until my pen is found we won't be able to allow outsiders in the house."

The next day Darren came home with his mother's pen. He reported that Brad said he had "borrowed" the pen to write something down and had "accidentally" put it in his pocket. Brad was then allowed to play with Darren in the house.

Mrs. T. handled a difficult situation very well. It would have been futile to try to persuade Brad to confess to the crime. By her action she gave Brad a chance to save face and fostered a good relationship with him, considerably reducing the chances of a repetition of the misbehavior in the future. However, if Brad does take something again, Mrs. T. can repeat her action.

Parents have a right to have their home and property respected. If other children violate the standards of one's home, then they must be told what is expected. Remaining calm, and utilizing the logical consequences of not allowing the children to play in the house if they misbehave, often decreases the incidence of misbehavior. But it is always important that the children be given another chance to prove that they can follow the rules.

PEER RELATIONSHIPS

When a child has difficulty making friends or getting along with peers, parents are naturally concerned. What parents do not realize is that the child must learn on his own how to get along with others. Parental interference in the child's peer relationships often only makes the situation worse.

Perhaps the most destructive response is feeling sorry for the child who exhibits difficulty in the social-relations area. Pity allows the child to feel that he is incapable of handling the situation, and he easily convinces himself that there is nothing to do about the problem except join his parents in feeling sorry. Children who have peer-relationship problems, like all other discouraged children, need encouragement, not pity.

Several afternoons a week nine-year-old Joe would get beaten up at the school bus stop. Joe would run home crying. Joe's mother felt sorry for him and was quite angry with the other children. Father, on the other hand, felt that Joe needed to be a "man" and learn to fight back. But he, too, became disgusted and angry after one of Joe's fights and called all the fathers of the boys involved, demanding that they do something about their sons' treatment of Joe.

For a few days Joe wasn't attacked. He did get teased quite severely, however. He reported the teasing to Mother, who again felt sorry for the unfortunate waif. Father told him to ignore the teasing.

A week later the threats of the other fathers had worn off and the boys again attacked Joe.

When parents feel sorry for a child they tend to be overprotective and rob him of the experience of developing social skills. Pity, lectures on being a "man," demanding action from other boys' fathers, and advice to ignore teasing did not aid Joe in his dilemma. Joe does not intend to fight back or ignore the boys, for he has discovered a good way to gain attention and sympathy. He makes his parents fight his battles by being "weak and incapable" of taking care of himself.

Joe will learn to handle his peer problems only when his parents let him. If they are going to help their son, they must refrain from pity, advice, and overprotection. When Joe comes home with a tale of woe, Mother must stop pampering him and begin to help Joe work through his feelings and consider alternatives.

When it is explained to parents that children must learn to fight their own battles, many parents will agree as long as the children involved are about the same age. But what about older children who pick on younger children? Just as younger siblings must learn to survive the problems of older siblings, younger children must learn how to fend for themselves. In fact, often the younger child's "underdog" status is a ploy. By antagonizing older children to the point where they use physical means to stop them, many younger children gain much-desired attention and sympathy from their parents.

> Tommy, age five, and Jerry, age eight, were watching television in the family room. Tommy began to tease Jerry by waving his hand in front of Jerry's face while Jerry was intently trying to watch the program. Jerry kept telling Tommy to stop, but Tommy continued.
>
> Jerry tried holding Tommy's hand still, but Tommy would struggle free and continue. Finally Jerry had had enough and he hit Tommy. Tommy let out a loud yell and began crying. Mother came running from the back of the house. "What happened?" she demanded. Tommy cried, "He hit me!" Jerry complained, "Well, I was trying to—" "I don't care," said Mother angrily, "you know you're not supposed to hit your little brother. You go to your room!"
>
> Then Mother turned to Tommy and said comfortingly, "Now, now, it will be all right, honey."

Mother has been trapped. Tommy knows exactly how to get his mother's attention! He can do anything he wants to Jerry and Mother will support him. Mother doesn't realize how she contributes to the discouragement of both her sons. She discourages Jerry by punishing him for trying to defend his own rights. He may come to feel that Tommy is favored. His desire to get even with Tommy, and with Mother, may create more problems as he grows older. In addition to discouraging Jerry, she cripples Tommy, who may learn to believe: "I have a right to do what I want, and others will protect me when I get myself into difficulty." If Mother would not interfere, Tommy would soon learn not to tease his brother.

In some situations a younger child could become seriously

hurt—for example, if there is a great age discrepancy, or if there is a severely disturbed youngster involved. Under these circumstances parents may need to use forceful restrictions, or, in the case of a neighbor's child, they may have to call the older or disturbed child's parents and ask them to keep the child at home.

Parents who are concerned with "bad" influences often create battlegrounds over their child's choice of friends. Overconcern and attempts to prevent a child from playing with whom he chooses often increase the child's desire to choose such companions. In addition, trying to choose a child's friends denies him necessary experiences, for children must learn to deal with all kinds of people.

Chuck had just moved into the neighborhood. He was quite belligerent and disrespectful, and he showed no regard for the property of others. After a few days it was obvious to all the parents that the newcomer was not the kind of boy they wished their children to become involved with.

Mr. and Mrs. Z.'s son, Jeff, age ten, had struck up a friendship with the new boy. Both parents told their son that they did not think his new friend was a very good boy and that they did not want Jeff to associate with him anymore. Jeff stated that he could not understand why they felt that way and that he resented their interference in his affairs. Mr. and Mrs. Z. became quite angry and warned Jeff not to associate with Chuck again. The session ended with much ill feeling between Jeff and his parents.

The next day Jeff did not come home after school at the usual time. When he finally arrived, Mother asked him where he had been. Jeff said that he and some other boys had decided to play baseball on the playground after school. Mother asked who was there. Jeff replied, "Oh, just some of the guys." Mother asked him to name the other youngsters. Jeff angrily named a few of his friends. Because of Jeff's reluctance to answer, Mother suspected that he was not telling the truth. She asked, "Was Chuck there?" "No," Jeff said sheepishly. "I don't think you're telling me the truth," replied Mother.

"I don't care what you think!" Jeff snarled in return. "Don't talk to me like that," yelled Mother. "You just wait till your father gets home!"

When Father found out what had transpired between Jeff and his mother, he gave Jeff the third degree. "All right," cried Jeff, "I was with Chuck. He's my friend, and I'm going to play with him if I want to!" At this point Father lost his temper and gave Jeff a good spanking.

Mr. and Mrs. Z. have embarked on a futile course. Short of keeping Jeff in the house day and night, what can they possibly do to keep him from playing with Chuck? Jeff's desire and determination to associate with the black sheep of the neighborhood has been increased by his parents' reaction. It is obvious that Mr. and Mrs. Z. need to work on their relationship with their son. What action can they take in this situation?

They will need to ask Jeff what he values in his relationship with Chuck. They just might discover that they have been too hasty in their evaluation of Chuck.

If we want children to internalize a set of values about many things, including human relationships, we must let them learn from experience. Children are not helped to grow by adopting our unquestioned standards and opinions.

A child who has no friends presents a problem.

Mrs. N. was greatly concerned because her daughter, Paula, age eight, had no friends. After school and on weekends Paula would stay around the house by herself. Mrs. N. talked with her a great deal about getting out and associating with others. Mother would often make her go outside to play, but Paula very seldom left the yard.

Mother coaxed her daughter into calling various girls in the neighborhood. Once in a while Paula would succeed in inviting a playmate to come over. The play time was usually short, however, as Paula did not seem to be very much fun to play with.

After the other child had left, Mrs. N. would lecture her daughter about why she had not succeeded in keeping her friend interested in playing. Paula listened very patiently, but the situation did not change.

What Mrs. N. does not realize is that at this point Paula really has no need for friends of her own age—she has her mother! Paula has discovered a clever way of keeping Mother busy worrying, talking, and coaxing. She gains so much attention from Mother by not having friends that she would be foolish to make friends. When Mother decides to put the responsibility for friendship on her daughter's shoulders and refuses to talk about it and plan remedies, when she ceases to be concerned, Paula will very likely discover that remaining a loner is not too beneficial.

Parents must realize that they cannot interfere in their children's peer relations if they wish them to develop adequate social skills. Feeling sorry, fighting battles, lecturing, forbidding associations, and trying to get children to associate with others all discourage favorable development. Children learn to deal with others when they are allowed to. Interference only hampers the process.

DANGER

In danger or emergency situations it is obvious that one cannot allow the child to experience the natural consequences of his behavior. Logical consequences, however, can still be used.

> Eight-month-old Grant was crawling on the living room floor. In his curiosity he began to touch the wall socket. Mother jumped up from her chair, grabbed Grant, and gave him a swat, saying, "No, no."
> A few minutes later Grant again approached the socket. Again Mother grabbed him, spanked, and yelled. She then put Grant in his playpen.

Little Grant certainly did not enjoy being spanked, but it appears he enjoyed the attention he received from Mother by

his actions! Why didn't Mother simply put Grant in his play-
pen the first time he touched the outlet? Certainly Mother did
not want Grant to be hurt, but from her reaction it seems that
she also had another motive—teaching Grant to mind her.
Again, "Do what I say because I say it" is usually ineffective. If
Mother wants to teach Grant to leave the outlets alone, she
will have to change her approach.

> Eight-month-old Grant was crawling on the living room
> floor. In his curiosity he began to touch the wall socket.
> Mother picked Grant up and placed him in his playpen.
> A few minutes later she took him out of the pen. Grant
> crawled around and again approached the outlet. Mother
> again placed him in the pen, but this time she left him in for
> a longer time. When Grant was let out again he amused him-
> self with a toy.

By her action Mother has shown Grant that if he wishes to
have the freedom of the living room he must stay away from
the wall socket. He responded favorably because he gained no
attention from his misbehavior as he had in the first example.
But his freedom of movement was restricted, and little Grant
decided he would rather be outside the pen than play with the
socket.

> It was a nice day, and Tammi, age four, wanted to play
> outside. Mother told her that she could go outside as long as
> she stayed in the yard. She then explained to Tammi that she
> did not want her to go into the street because she might get
> hit by a car.
> A few minutes later she noticed that Tammi had ventured
> into the street. Mother came from the house and led Tammi
> by the hand back into the yard. She then asked her daughter,
> "Would you like to play in the yard or would you like to play
> in the house?" Tammi replied that she would rather play in
> the yard. Mother then went back into the house and watched
> Tammi from the window. Tammi played in the yard for a few
> minutes and then stepped into the street. Mother went out-
> side and said to Tammi, "I see that you have decided to play

in the house. You can go outside later, and then we'll see if you are ready to stay in the yard." Tammi began to cry and said that she did not want to come in. Mother said, "Do you want to come in on your own or shall I help you?" Tammi made no response. Mother then took her by the hand and led her into the house.

About a half hour later Tammi asked Mother if she could play outside in the yard again. Mother replied, "Not right now. We'll try a little later to see if you are ready." About ten minutes later Tammi asked again and Mother said yes. Mother again watched from the window. Tammi seemed to be content to play in the yard. A while later, however, Mother looked out the window and saw that Tammi was again in the street. Mother went outside, took Tammi by the hand, and led her into the house. When they reached the house Mother said, "We will try again tomorrow, Tammi."

Here Mother has approached the problem in a matter-of-fact way. She remained calm, gave Tammi a choice, and acted on Tammi's decision. Mother was both firm and kind.

If, after receiving another chance the following day, Tammi still goes into the street, Mother will have to restrict her from the yard for a longer time.

BED-WETTING

Bed-wetting can be a particularly difficult problem. Usually the problem accelerates and maintains itself in proportion to the increasing concern of the parent.

The first step involves determining if bed-wetting should be regarded as a problem. Children differ in their readiness for bladder control. Unless the child has been able to remain dry for several consecutive nights, it may indicate that he is not ready and still needs diapers. If he has passed that stage and the bed-wetting suggests a regression, the parent should check with his physician to determine if there is any organic or structural problem. Experience indicates that most cases are functional, not structural. It is foolish, however, to apply special methods to a problem that is essentially physical.

Most children who are involved in the problem have become aware that bed-wetting is a powerful tool. Thus one begins by checking if the parent-child relationship is good or if the child is doing this to control, get even, or obtain special service or attention.

Do not fuss, take note of it constantly, threaten, retaliate, or give the child unnecessary service because of the problem. Attention sustains the problem. It is important that the parent check to make certain that he is not applying too much pressure in certain areas for which the child may be using bed-wetting to retaliate.

The parent can best handle the problem by indicating that he understands the child's feelings about the accident—that he is embarrassed, or feels foolish—and that he understands how much the child would like to stop. If the child senses this kind of parental support, it may be possible to explore some solutions together.

If joint efforts fail, then the parent may want to have the child become responsible for changing his sheets. In certain instances the parent can approach the child in a friendly fashion, explaining that he knows the bed-wetting is not intentional, and putting him back in training pants until such time as he indicates he does not need the special clothing.

Bed-wetting can become complicated, so avoid making it a major concern. Apply logical consequences, and if it continues, consult a professional who works with childhood problems.

CHAPTER 8

Games Children Play

The games children play are social methods for getting their way or achieving their goals. Often the product of a poor parent-child relationship and limited mutual respect, they are best understood in terms of their purpose. Games make sense to the one who starts the game. The purpose of the game can usually be determined by noting the consequences or the response of the adult involved. If he is annoyed, seeks to control, is irrationally angry or defeated, this may be exactly what the child wants to achieve.

Games require as few as two participants—the child and the victim. They may occur in response to tasks or social relationships. Their targets are parents, teachers, siblings, other children, or innocent bystanders. The games are usually enjoyed by the child, but dreaded by the victim. Some games are learned by observing older siblings, other children, or by watching the social transaction between parents or between parents and the child. They may even be culturally acceptable in the family, "Oh, he's only a child," "After all, he is the youngest," "It's a stage he's going through," or "All boys fight."

Games usually have established roles and represent an unsigned contract between the child and the victim. The child expects the other participant to react in a certain way, and he is rarely disappointed. In an argument between a child and his parent, each is convinced that he is right and instead of working out a solution, they have agreed to fight. When one of them—usually the parent—stops arguing, the agreement is broken. The child cannot continue the game without an opponent.

The most interesting part of the game is that the child is usually the only one who knows the rules and how to keep score. Hence he is inevitably the winner. In any game between parent and child, if the parent alters his approach and presents the child with an unexpected reaction, the game usually stops. The child who whines and cries each time things do not go his way expects the parent to react in a certain manner—with hostility and punishment, for example. If the parent becomes familiar with our rationale and corrective procedures presented in the ensuing section, he will be able to participate in the games with proper equipment.

SHOCKIE

Shockie is played by a child who uses vulgar language and backtalk to force a reaction from his opponent, the parent. The child scores points by proving he is strong, horrible, and uncontrollable. The defense loses points by commanding, lecturing, moralizing, and can only succeed in stopping the game by doing the opposite of whatever the child expects.

Children often hear vulgar words from their peers. Children who do not know a word is unacceptable or "bad" may innocently repeat it in the presence of parents. Most parents overreact to "bad" language, causing the child to discover that the word has value in terms of gaining attention, proving how big he is, or effectively striking back at his parents. Children who are aware of the inappropriateness of the word may use it for the same purposes. Its shock value makes it very useful for achieving a desired result.

Parents who complain about swearing are frequently guilty of the same offense, and often in front of their children! Today's children do not accept double standards, feeling that if parents have a right to swear, so have they. In addition, they often begin to equate such behavior with being grown up. (Even if parents do not swear, there is no guarantee that their children will not choose to use the words for the same shock value that other children discover.)

There are several methods to stop the game of Shockie. If the parent is unimpressed by a swear word, it will probably lose its shock value, and its use will become less frequent or stop completely. Or the parent can utilize the following suggestion:

> Jay, age nine, and his sister Pam, age eight, were playing in the woods one day where some older children were using four-letter words. On returning home the children began using some of the words in the presence of their mother. Mother calmly asked the children if they knew the meaning of the words. When she found they did not, she took time to explain their meanings. After the discussion Mother requested them not to use such words in her presence. Her request was respected.

This mother did not allow herself to be trapped by her children. She approached the problem in a calm, matter-of-fact way. She did not condemn her children, but showed them respect, making a learning experience out of a situation that others night have found intolerable. Her request was respected as a result of her approach to the problem.

Backtalk is similar to swearing in its effect. Parents become highly insulted when their child expresses an angry, hostile feeling toward them, viewing it as lack of respect. In fact, many parents and teachers often complain that children today do not respect adults. What these parents and teachers fail to realize is that respect must be mutual. Adults think nothing of yelling, insulting, threatening, and punishing children, while at the same time they insist the children should respect their elders. The double standard of respect is not accepted by children today. Today's child feels that he is just as much entitled to respect as his parents or teacher.

When an adult behaves disrespectfully toward a child because of anger or frustration, he expects the child to excuse him, for after all, he is only human. Yet when a child displays similar behavior, he is rarely shown the same tolerance. If we adults wish to be shown respect by our children, then we must extend respect, and we must eliminate criticisms and admonishments from our relationships with them.

When a child is disrespectful, his parent should examine his own behavior. Has he been respectful to the child? If the answer is no, then the parent will have to concentrate on correcting his own behavior. If, however, the parent feels he has been respectful, he should *allow the child to be human.*

> Pattie, age seven, was very angry with her mother for not allowing her to stay overnight with a friend on a school night. "The other mothers allow their children to do this. You're just mean. I wish you weren't my mother," sobbed Pattie. Following previous outbursts such as this, Pattie would usually receive a spanking and be sent to bed. This time, however, Mother had decided to try a new approach. She simply said, "I understand you are angry and I appreciate how you feel." Pattie, very much surprised by her mother's reaction, quieted down, and the rest of the evening was spent pleasantly.

This mother realized Pattie's right to feel angry and deprived of something that she wished to do. She also realized that returning anger and punishment would only make the situation worse. Mother used reflective listening and succeeded in winning Pattie over.

There are other ways in which the parent can react to the child when he attempts to hurt the parent's feelings. Sometimes it is sufficient to agree with him by saying, "You're probably right," or "You have a right to feel that way." At other times it is best to say nothing and be unimpressed by the child's remarks. When the child talks back, his intent is to get even. He expects anger and retaliation or hurt feelings in return. But his game is futile unless the parent cooperates with him by doing what he expects. The unexpected reaction often stops the child's act and helps establish a more effective relationship.

HE STARTED IT

This game requires at least two children who decide to "square off" and settle their differences on the field of battle. In addition, there must be a referee on the scene who is not familiar with the rules of combat. The referee must interfere constantly or the game cannot continue. Therefore, if the parent is referee and wishes to discontinue this game, he should hand in his resignation.

Fighting among siblings is so common that it is often accepted as normal. But this is certainly not the case. Like all child misbehavior, fighting is purposive. Some children fight to gain attention from parents, others to show parents that they can do what they want, even in defiance of their parents' wishes. And some children pick on a favored child to seek revenge on parents. Our expectations play such an important role in children's fighting that we accept fighting as normal and *expect* them to fight; children make a special effort not to let us down. Many of us set examples of human relationships filled with fighting. We fight with our spouse, neighbors, and children, and our children follow our example. In some families fighting is almost a family value.

Children learn not to fight only when the parent refuses to become involved in the squabbles. Parent involvement in sibling rivalries only increases the conflict. No matter how objective the parent feels he is, from at least one child's point of view, and perhaps from all of them, he is unfair. When the parent decides to place the responsibility for learning how to get along with others on the children's shoulders, they learn that fighting only brings discomfort. The fighting may worsen during initial testing in order that the children may see if the parent really intends to remain uninvolved, but then it will begin to decrease in frequency and intensity.

Many parents feel that although it is permissible for boys to fight with each other, they should not hit girls. This double standard creates much friction in a family of brothers and sisters. Many girls take full advantage of attitudes about the "weakness" of their sex and begin to strike their brothers as soon as they discover that boys are not allowed to hit back. But girls soon learn not to pick on their brothers when the parents decide not to interfere in the battles.

Some parents find it difficult to let older children fight with younger siblings. They feel the young ones are weaker and can't take care of themselves. This is a definite misconception. Many younger siblings provoke those who are older simply to win the parents over to their side. They use the parent as a weapon to control the older one. Parental protection of the younger child often contributes to a poor relationship between the younger and older siblings, as well as between the older siblings and the parents. It is only when the parent refuses to interfere and refuses to protect the younger child that little brothers or sisters learn to stop provoking the older ones. Of course at first they intensify their efforts to force the parent back into the protecting role, but if the parent maintains his position of noninterference, the little one will usually decide it isn't beneficial to provoke the older brother or sister.

When parents decide to disengage themselves from sibling arguments, they often will find one child attempting to get them involved again by tattling. When this happens the child must be told that the problem is between himself and his brother or sister and the parent is confident the child can handle it. The parent avoids playing the role of judge and simultaneously instills the child with faith in his own problem-solving abilities. Children don't like this approach and may try all kinds of tricks to coax the parent back into the game. Some children go so far as to get "injured" in an effort to play on the parent's protective desires.

With the exception of severely disturbed youngsters, most siblings have mixed feelings about each other and will not really hurt one another in a fight. But some children resort to using objects that could accidentally injure a sibling. When this happens, it is best to remove the objects and inform the children that if they wish to fight they will have to use their hands. This unexpected reaction confuses the children, and although they may make several more attempts to provoke a desired reaction, if the parent remains firm in his decision the situation will most likely soon begin to improve.

Children have a right to fight, but the location of the battle is open to some consideration. When they are fighting in their own rooms or in other areas acceptable to the parent, the parent can remove himself without any comment. He may go to his bedroom, lock the door, and turn on a radio, emerging after the storm has passed. Some parents find it helpful to take a walk when the children begin to fight.

However, if they are fighting in areas that are dangerous, or if they are endangering family property, the parent can inform them that they can fight if they wish, but they will have to fight in whatever spot the parent designates. Often this action alone will stop the fight. By not denying the children the right to fight, and by refusing to become involved and stop the battle, the purpose of the fight cannot be achieved. But as soon as the parent misuses this approach in an attempt to "make" the children stop fighting, failure is likely. Attitude is most important.

FRAGILE—HANDLE WITH CARE

A child who plays this game must have very thin skin. He walks around with a long chin, drooping mouth, and teary eyes. He looks as if the dam will burst any second! His behavior says, "I require special treatment or I will break." His parents often feel as if they are walking on eggs—one false move and . . . ! He controls everybody; his feelings are his power. Parents end this game when they stop being overconcerned with the child's feelings and respect themselves enough to do what they think is necessary.

Sensitive people are often quite unhappy. As they try to control others they experience resistance and often rejection. Sensitive children get hurt easily and are often the targets of teasing. Others feel uncomfortable around overly sensitive people, fearing that they might hurt their feelings.

If the parent treats a sensitive child with special care, he misses opportunities to help the child learn to give and take and at the same time handle his feelings. Overconcern with how the child might feel about a necessary action blocks opportunities for communication and hinders the child's development.

CATCH ME, I BEG YOU

This game requires a "criminal" and a "detective." The "criminal" leaves clues to a "crime," usually making sure the "detective" solves the "crime." Lying, sneaking, stealing are methods employed by the "criminal." When the "detective" decides not to make the arrest, the "criminal" usually becomes tired of the game.

In Catch Me the child is "clumsy" enough so that he is discovered. If he isn't caught, the game may be over. If he is caught and denies the act, it may be a way to ensure further parental involvement.

Lying and stealing are two forms of behavior that are most disturbing to parents. They feel that unless they promptly put a stop to such behavior the child will degenerate into a pathological liar or a thief. The moral aspects of these acts often cause a parent to react quite severely to the culprit.

One must realize that all children lie at some time in their childhood. Most children have also taken things that don't belong to them at one time or another. These occasional misdeeds do not make a child a liar or a thief. The most dangerous aspects of lying and stealing are not the actions themselves but the reactions of the parents! Parents who treat their transgressor as a dishonest person stand a good chance of producing one.

Many times parents unintentionally encourage children to lie by using punishment. When the child misbehaves he may lie to avoid being punished. But when the child is allowed to experience consequences, lying becomes unnecessary.

LYING

Some children lie when the truth is obvious to everyone.

> Kathy asked Mother if she could have some cookies. Because they would spoil her dinner, Mother denied her request.
>
> Mother went to her room for a few minutes. When she returned she saw Kathy watching television, chocolate cookie crumbs obvious around her mouth.
>
> "I thought I told you not to have cookies?"
>
> "I didn't," said Kathy.
>
> "Then why do you have crumbs all over your face?" asked Mother.
>
> "Oh," said Kathy, quickly wiping the crumbs off her face.
>
> "I don't like to be lied to. So just for that, young lady, you can go to bed without your supper."

It is obvious that Kathy did not intend to try to keep secrets from Mother, for she could have destroyed the evidence. Why would a child lie when the evidence is so apparent? In this case it seems that Kathy has learned that she can gain attention from her lies. If she did not "forget" to take care of the evidence, she could not gain the attention.

Let's suppose Mother acted as if Kathy had no crumbs on her face. Suppose she pretended that Kathy did not raid the cookie jar. If Mother did not give Kathy the opportunity to lie, she would gain no attention from "cookie crumbs on the face" behavior. After a few tries Kathy would probably take "no" for an answer.

Some children may use behavior such as Kathy's for the purpose of power or revenge. In these cases the parents may have to lock up things while refraining from playing detective and punishing.

In some situations lying cannot be ignored.

> Eight-year-old Brad told his mother he was going to Jimmy's house. At about four o'clock Mother called Jimmy's mother, Mrs. A., to ask her to send Brad home. Mrs. A. said that Brad was not there and had not been at her house or playing with Jimmy all day.
>
> In a few minutes Brad came home. "Where have you been?" demanded Mother. "At Jimmy's," Brad replied nervously.
>
> "Don't you lie to me! I just called Mrs. A. and she said you haven't been there all day. Now, where were you?"

Mother's decision to give Brad the third degree is no guarantee that she will get a truthful answer or that he will not lie in the future. In fact, her action may increase Brad's lying. It appears that Brad has decided to show his mother, by his lies, that he intends to do only what *he* wants to do. Mother is determined to prove that he can't, and thus we have a power contest. Suppose Mother had handled the situation thus:

> When Brad came home Mother made no comment about where he had actually gone. However, the next day when Brad approached Mother to tell her he was going someplace, Mother said, "I'm sorry, Brad, but yesterday you did not go to Jimmy's as you had said you would. Therefore you will have to stay home today, and tomorrow we will see if you are ready to go out on your own."

With this approach Mother has kept her control. She has been firm but kind, without accusing or moralizing. And she has offered Brad another chance to prove his trustworthiness. Her chances of influencing him are much better.

> Mr. and Mrs. J. went to the store one afternoon, leaving Judy, ten, and Greg, nine, at home. When they returned they found a lamp broken. Mr. J. asked the children, "What happened to the lamp?"
>
> Judy answered, "I don't know. Greg must have broken it."
> "I did not. You did."
>
> The children continued to argue, each proclaiming his own innocence and accusing the other. Mr. J. interrupted them, "I'm sorry, but I have no way of knowing who did this, so you will both have to pay for it out of your allowance."
>
> Both children complained bitterly, but Mr. J. did not argue. "Now, how shall we arrange payment? The lamp cost twenty dollars. How much do each of you wish to pay out of your weekly allowances?" The children still complained, but Mr. J. went on as if they were not complaining, proposing ways they could pay for it. Finally the children calmed down and made arrangements to pay.

While this approach may seem unfair to the innocent one, Mr. J. had no alternative but to make both responsible. Since the children could not get Dad to play detective or to take sides, they finally settled down and took the consequences.

Some children's lies take the form of exaggeration or tall tales.

> Sandy, eleven, would often irritate her parents by exaggerating and stretching the truth. They would usually respond to her proclamations with such comments as "You know that's not true" or "Oh, come on, who do you think you're kidding?" Sandy would then elaborately defend her statements. The session normally ended with resentment and the continuance of a poor relationship.

What Sandy's parents don't realize is that her exaggerations are symptoms of a deeper discouragement. It appears that

Sandy does not feel she can gain a place through useful contributions, so she gains the attention and recognition she desires through useless tales.

If they wish to help her, Sandy's parents should stop reinforcing her misbehavior. They simply can listen, refraining from negative comment or nonverbal cues, when she decides to exaggerate. Facial expression will be of utmost importance. If her parents show through their body language that they disapprove of Sandy, they will be reinforcing the behavior.

If silence is not effective, Sandy's parents could help her understand her purpose by reflecting, "It seems that you feel it's important to impress us." If a discussion follows, the parents can employ their reflective listening skills and help Sandy reconsider the importance of being overconcerned with impressing others. They can help her explore the possibility of recognition for positive contributions, and then find ways for Sandy to establish a place by being useful. They can begin by capitalizing on her best contributions to the family.

STEALING

How a parent reacts when a child steals often helps to determine the child's view of himself as an honest or dishonest person.

> While cleaning seven-year-old Mike's room Mother discovered a baseball glove that she knew was not his. She approached Mike with, "Where did you get this glove?"
>
> "I borrowed it from Tommy."
>
> Mother could tell from Mike's facial expression that "borrow" was not the proper word.
>
> "You mean you stole it, don't you?" asked Mother angrily.
>
> Mike hung his head and did not answer.
>
> "Now, listen here, young man, you know stealing is *very* wrong. You just march down to Tommy's and give it back to him this minute!"

While Mother may have been successful in forcing Mike to return the glove, her action did not help her relationship with her son. Lecturing and making him feel like a thief certainly caused Mike to be resentful and does not guarantee that he will not repeat the behavior in the future.

Let's suppose Mother had used a different approach.

When Mike said that he had borrowed the baseball glove she discovered, Mother replied, "I guess you'll have to take it back to him. He'll probably be needing it."

Mother has refrained from playing detective. She acted as if she believed Mike and simply suggested he return the glove. There was no need for Mike to become defensive and resentful, since Mother handled the situation in a friendly manner. There was no need to lecture Mike on the evils of stealing—he knows stealing is wrong. Since he received no reinforcement for his misbehavior, Mike will probably stop "borrowing."

Mr. Y. noticed that some of his change was missing from his dresser top. He asked other family members if they knew what had happened to it. Everyone denied knowledge of its whereabouts.

The next day while preparing the clothes for washing, Mrs. Y. found some loose change in ten-year-old Bob's pocket. On questioning him about the money, he announced that he had found it on the school playground.

"I don't believe you, Bob. This is just about the same amount that Dad is missing. You stole this from Dad, didn't you?"

"Yes," replied Bob nervously.

"What did you do with the rest of it?"

"I bought some candy."

"You just wait until your father gets home. You really are going to get it. The very idea of stealing from your own father!"

When Father returned home he spanked Bob, declaring that he would not have a thief in his home.

Mother has made several errors. First, she moralized and lectured to Bob. Second, she interfered in a problem really belonging to Bob and his father. Third, since she had chosen to interfere, it was a mistake to threaten Bob with his father's anger instead of handling the situation herself. Father added to Bob's discouragement by punishing and name-calling. These actions are almost guaranteed to bring resentment and possible retaliation from Bob.

Let's see what might have happened if the situation had been handled differently.

> . . . The next day Mrs. Y. found some loose change in ten-year-old Bob's pocket. She said nothing to Bob, but instead waited until Mr. Y. came home. She then told her husband what she had found.
>
> Mr. Y. approached Bob. "Son, it appears that you have my missing change. If you feel you need more money, we can discuss a raise in your allowance or a plan for you to earn some extra money, but right now I'd like to have my change back. Also, we have to discuss how you will pay back the money you spent."

Here Bob's parents have approached the problem in a more positive way, and their chances of influencing Bob are much greater. Mother has refrained from interfering, and Father has refused to punish and lecture. Instead, he has offered his son a chance to discuss how he can *honestly* obtain more money, at the same time making his son responsible for returning all the money he took.

> Mr. and Mrs. C. and their three children went to the plaza. While in the department store, eleven-year-old June said she wanted to look around in the girls' clothing department. Mother agreed, telling June to meet them at the snack bar for lunch in about fifteen minutes.
>
> Two days later Mother was looking for a pair of slacks that needed mending. She happened to see a blouse in June's closet that had never been there before. Then she remembered how

extremely quiet June had been at lunch and on the way home after the trip to the plaza. And she remembered how anxious to get to her room June had been.

"June," said Mother, "where did you get this blouse?"

June's face reddened. "I bought it at the store the other day."

"I'm sorry, June, but I know how much this blouse costs, and you didn't have the money. What do you think should be done about this?"

June shrugged her shoulders and made no reply.

Mother said, "I think this is really between you and the store manager, so we'll go back to the store and you can talk to him about it."

Mother has approached a difficult problem in a positive way. It is probable that experiencing the embarrassment of facing the store manager will help June learn from her mistake.

If lying or stealing become severe or persistent, parents should seek the counsel of a professional, as they may be symptoms of a more serious difficulty.

CUSTER'S LAST STAND

This is one of the most intense and serious games in which parents and children can become engaged. The child gives his full involvement to the game because so much is at stake. Like Custer, he is desperate and determined. The game often occurs when the parents, through retraining, have learned to avoid many of the traps previously set by the child and the child reacts by making desperate attempts to re-establish his place.

Expressions such as "I hate you" and "You don't love me" are often utilized in the game. Other weapons are extremely "bad" and defiant behavior. Frequently the words or acts used have not been previously heard or witnessed by the parents. The child often succeeds in bringing about a relapse by catching the parents off guard.

Custer's Last Stand is not necessarily a final display of mis-behavior, but usually something that occurs and reoccurs in the relationship with the child. As the relationship improves, this behavior will decrease.

> After Mother had denied fifteen-year-old Ann's request for money to purchase the latest item of clothing on the market, Ann went into a fit of rage. "You're awful—you never let me do anything. I hate you!"
>
> Mother replied angrily, "Don't you dare talk to me that way. I've a good mind to slap your face, young lady!"
>
> Ann burst into tears and ran to her room, slamming the door.

Mother felt hurt and rejected by Ann's attack, so she coun-terattacked in an attempt to hurt Ann. This approach certainly will not help Ann learn to accept disappointments. Instead, she will probably feel cheated and even more entitled to get her way. It is difficult for the parent to remain calm when he feels unjustly attacked by the child. However, making the child feel hurt in return usually only invites further retaliation.

To render an insult or angry verbal attack ineffective, the parent can leave the situation whenever possible, agree with the child, or recognize his feelings. If Mother had kept her control, perhaps the situation would have been different.

> . . . Ann went into a fit of rage: "You're awful—you never let me do anything. I hate you!"
>
> Mother replied, "I know you're *really* angry with me and feel that I'm too restrictive, but I feel that I must limit money for clothing."
>
> Ann went to her room. Mother then returned to fixing supper, and when supper was ready she called Ann to the table. Ann came, but remained silent. Mother struck up a friendly conversation about the activities of a club to which Ann be-longed. Although Ann was slow to respond, Mother continued patiently until, after a short time, Ann joined the conversa-tion. A few minutes later Ann said, "I'm sorry I said what I did, Mom."

"I know," said Mother. "We all get angry and say things we don't mean. Let's forget about it, okay?"

"Okay," replied Ann with a smile.

Mother has managed to handle Ann's attack effectively without provoking further hostility. She recognized Ann's feelings and stated her own feelings and position. She refused to lecture Ann about respecting her mother, recognized Ann's right to be angry, and acknowledged that anger is a normal emotion that we sometimes express in ways we regret.

It is difficult to predict the type of "bad" or defiant behavior the child may choose to catch his parents off guard. The act or acts depend on the individual child and the particular family situation. When the parent experiences Custer's-Last-Stand behavior, he can apply what he has learned from this book:

Withdraw from conflict.

Avoid punishment.

Recognize feelings.

Send "I Messages."

Use encouragement.

Use natural and logical consequences.

Act—don't react.

TIME OUT FOR A SPECIAL BULLETIN

"Extra, extra, hear all about it!" shouts the family news reporter as his parents come into view. "Sally did this, Jimmy did that . . ." He rambles on and on. At this moment, if they are to stop the game, the parents must become "child deaf" and tune out the broadcast.

Paying attention to tattling is perhaps one of the most discouraging things the parent can do, since sibling rivalry and competition are increased by the parent's involvement in relationships between brothers and sisters. Most parents have at least one child whom they feel they can trust, and others whom they feel they cannot trust. When the trustworthy one tells them what happened or "who done it," they tend to accept his interpretation, although this acceptance may not be articulated. This is very discouraging to the child who is judged "guilty," for he cannot help but feel that his trustworthy sibling has a corner on the market of goodness, a value held in high esteem by most parents.

The trustworthy child, who has to flaunt his goodness by making others look bad, is often highly discouraged. When he cannot prove how good he is, he feels worthless. He suffers from inferiority feelings, as do his not-so-good brothers and sisters. Both his discouragement and his inferiority feelings are reinforced whenever the parent pays attention to his tattling behavior, for he wins his parent's approval by discrediting others. And he continues to feel that there is no more legitimate way for him to gain parental favor.

Many tattling situations are quite similar to fighting or bickering situations.

> Betty, age eight, and Terry, age nine, were playing with their dolls. Suddenly Betty ran screaming into the kitchen. "Mommy, Mommy, Terry broke my doll." "Why did she break it?" asked Mother. "She wanted to play with it, and I didn't want her to, so she threw it against the wall," sobbed Betty.
>
> Mother rushed into the girls' room and promptly proceeded to scold Terry for her misdeed. "Terry, why did you break your sister's doll?" asked Mother angrily. "She's so selfish. She wants to play with all my dolls, but she won't let me play with any of hers," Terry replied indignantly. "That's no reason to break her doll. You know you aren't supposed to destroy things, especially those that don't belong to you. Now, apologize to your sister and give her one of your dolls to replace the one you broke," ordered Mother. Terry stomped out of the room.

Mother is correct in feeling that Terry should not break toys, but questioning "why" is futile, as children are often unaware of their motivation. Terry's response may not give the correct reason. Most important, Mother fails to realize that Tammy and Terry have a competitive relationship, and that she contributes to their ill feelings toward each other by listening to tattling and by interfering in their fights.

Parents must realize that there is usually not just one guilty party in a fight. All contestants share in the responsibility for the problem. Punishing one or all reinforces the poor relationship. Children must learn to get along together. This will happen when the parents do not interfere, but allow the children to learn through their own experience. No amount of preaching or scolding will help them develop healthy human relationships. Becoming involved in a detective game of "Who done it" will only ensure the parent's imprisonment by the child! Instead, Mother should have informed the tattler that the problem is between herself and her sister, and Mother can express confidence that the child can handle the situation.

> Peter, age ten, and Larry, age seven, expressed the wish to remain home rather than go on a shopping trip with Mother. Mother gave her permission and instructed the boys to remain in the house while she was at the store.
>
> After her shopping trip Peter told his mother that Larry had gone to a friend's house, but had managed to be home before her return.

Peter usually tattled on Larry when he disobeyed Mother's instructions. Larry knew that Peter would tattle this time, and he also knew that he would probably get in trouble, as he had in the past. Why, then, did he disobey Mother, knowing that he would end up in difficulty? There are several possible explanations. He may feel that this is the only way he can gain his mother's attention. Perhaps he feels he only has a place when he is the boss. Or he may feel that Peter is Mother's favorite, and so he punishes her by flagrant disobedience.

How should Mother handle the situation? Obviously, if she acts on Peter's information, she will contribute to Larry's discouragement. It is best, perhaps, to ignore Peter's bid for superiority and Larry's desire to invoke her wrath. This is another version of the incident:

> "Mom," said Peter, "Larry went to play with John after you told him not to." Larry looked sheepishly at his mother, awaiting her reply. Mother said, "Let's see, if we're going to have fish for dinner, I'd better get busy," and promptly left the room. Peter followed her, saying, "Mom, didn't you hear me? I said Larry disobeyed you and went to John's." Mother continued to prepare dinner without a word. After a few more tries Peter left the kitchen with a disgusted look on his face. Larry's astonishment was also quite evident.

It may seem unfair to Peter to ignore his comment on Larry's behavior. However, any reply Mother makes to Peter's information will contribute to the problem. Even if she says, I'm sorry, I don't listen to tattling," she has acknowledged the fact that she has, in fact, listened to the tattling! Therefore Mother has to train Peter and Larry through her silence. It will not be too long before Peter discovers that tattling is useless. And Larry may decide to stop trying to provoke Mother by depending on Peter's tattling habit when he sees Mother will not become involved. At the same time the relationship between the two brothers will be improved as both boys discover that Mother is not going to favor one over the other.

> Bob, thirteen, and Sharon, ten, were constantly bickering. Sharon habitually tattled on Bob, and Mother frequently acted on her information.
> After attending parent group sessions Mother decided that she would not get involved in their arguments or pay attention to tattling.
> One evening Mother was in her bedroom sewing. Sharon knocked on the door and entered. "Mom, Bob got himself a snack and left the table messy." "Okay," was Mother's only reply. "Mom, aren't you going to make him clean it up?" demanded Sharon. "I'm busy now, dear," answered her mother. Sharon looked at her in surprise and left the room.
> At about six-thirty the children discovered that dinner was

not ready and that Mother was in the family room watching TV. "Mom," said Sharon, "Why isn't dinner ready?" "I'm sorry, Sharon, but I don't like to cook in a messy kitchen." Both Bob and Sharon were confused by Mother's response. "Bob left it messy, he should clean it up," announced Sharon. "I'm sorry, but I was sewing most of the afternoon, and all I know is that the kitchen is messy," Mother said. "But I told you, Bob messed it up," Sharon replied in an annoyed tone. "I'm going to finish my sewing—you two figure out what should be done." And Mother promptly left the room. A few minutes later Sharon came to report that she and Bob had cleaned up the kitchen. Mother proceeded to cook.

The reader may be thinking, Isn't this unfair to Sharon? Why should she have to clean the kitchen when Bob made the mess? It may seem unfair until one remembers the dynamics of the children's behavior. Sharon is the "good" child, maintaining her image at Bob's expense. Bob may feel "ganged up on" by Mother and Sharon. The only way he can gain any recognition is probably by misbehaving. And Mother falls into his trap each time she listens to tattling.

To improve the relationship between Bob and Sharon, and between Bob and herself, Mother must refrain from discouraging Bob by getting involved in tattling. Once Sharon discovers that she cannot gain recognition through tattling she will probably stop. And when Bob realizes that Mother is not against him, that she does not take sides, he will probably feel better toward her and refrain from disobedience.

In this situation and many others the parent is a poor judge of who did what, as he was not "at the scene of the crime." Many parents find that when they approach the accused, they receive a flat denial of the misdeed. At such times it is best to place the responsiblity on the shoulders of all the children and avoid being trapped in the tattling game. Trying to find out "who did it" is usually a frustrating experience and fosters poor relationships between siblings as well as between parents and children.

Emergency or danger situations always must be attended to. But lecturing about the "whys" and "why nots" and punishing are usually just as ineffective in a danger situation as they are in other instances. In an emergency the prevention of harm is the most important consideration. And this requires action—not talk.

> Becky, age six, was playing with matches in her bedroom. Suddenly the wastepaper basket caught fire. Nine-year-old Tony ran to get Mother. Mother rushed into the room, saw the blaze, ran into the bathroom for a glass of water, and extinguished the fire. She then took the matches from Becky. She got Becky interested in one of her toys and then proceeded to place the family's supply of matches in a safe place in another room.

It is safe to assume that Becky was frightened by the fire. Mother's decision to treat the situation with action rather than the offender with lectures and scolding gave Becky the confidence that she could make a mistake, even a serious one, without experiencing rejection. Becky had probably been told at some time not to play with matches and that fire is dangerous. She now had the opportunity to experience this at first hand.

Some children will use danger situations to provoke parents. Thus Mother's use of precautionary measures was advisable, as she had no way of knowing whether Becky had learned her lesson from this one experience.

THE GREATEST SHOW ON EARTH

This game requires a child who follows in the footsteps of those who grace the silver screen. He is a method actor with a desire to *make* things go his way. His methods include stomping, screaming, crying, threatening, begging. His audience is dumbfounded, wondering what to do. At times they may attempt to placate him, or they may try to subdue him. Either way he wins—his audience reacts! When he is thwarted in his attempts, his performance equals academy-award quality. But when the audience leaves, the curtain falls.

Temper tantrums are power plays designed to force a parent to give in to the child's demands. But the success of the tantrum does not always depend on the parent's fulfillment of the child's wishes. Many parents do not give in, but rather become quite angry and punish the child. A hostile reaction may also serve to reinforce the child's purpose behind the tantrum. "If I can't have my way at least I can get you upset."

Seven-year-old Ray had a history of temper tantrums. Whenever things did not go his way he would scream, cry, and stamp his feet. Mother had tried everything from ignoring him to pleading, reasoning, and spanking. But nothing would cause the tantrums to cease.

She discussed the problem with a counselor, who explained that Ray knew how to get Mother upset. Whenever he didn't like a particular situation he would punish Mother for it. The counselor suggested that when Ray gave his next performance Mother should retire to her room, lock the door, turn up the radio, and read a magazine—or she might take a walk. He recommended that she shouldn't reappear until Ray was finished with his tantrum.

Mother reported that it took several trips to her room before Ray began to realize that his tantrums were wasted efforts. In fact, Ray even tried screaming and pounding and kicking her bedroom door. Mother did not respond—she just turned up her radio. After a short time the house began to become much more peaceful.

This mother and her dealings with a tyrannical child are quite typical. Most mothers attempt several methods in an effort to get the child to stop the tantrums. But the fact that Mother had "tried" to ignore Ray attests to how powerful he really was. Ray knew his mother could not succeed in her efforts to ignore him. All he had to do was to increase the intensity, and she would eventually react to his performance. It was only when Mother removed herself and placed a door between herself and Ray that she was able to convince him that she was no longer impressed by his behavior.

BROKEN RECORD

Broken Record requires a child who is "hard of hearing" and a parent who repeats herself at least ten times a day. The object of the game is to frustrate the parent by not listening. The longer the child keeps the parent involved in reminding and nagging, the more points scored. In fact, maximum points are scored if he can manage to remain temporarily "deaf" until the parent gives up. This game ends rather quickly if the parent turns off the phonograph and turns on the action!

Many parents talk more than is necessary to be effective. There is little that can be accomplished through a continuous flow of words if the intention is to influence the child. We are in favor of communication, but it should be mutual, through which both parent and child hear each other's feelings and conflict-resolution procedures are used.

The parent must eliminate his critical comments and substitute natural and logical consequences in order to influence the child. Children generally learn best when they experience the unpleasant results of their misbehavior. Parents are advised to remember the old expression "Actions speak louder than words."

MY TIME IS SLOW TIME

My Time Is Slow Time is played by the child who is very skilled at delaying his parents when they are ready to leave. Repetitions of "Aren't you ready yet?" and "We're going to leave you home next time" are heard echoing down the halls. All such attempts are usually met with increased slowness.

Double time is generally achieved when the parents decide to invest money in a baby-sitter.

Parents who continue to wait for the child when he is not ready often give the child the impression that although "time waits for no man," it waits for him. The child must learn to plan effectively so that he can be on time. Most adults know how much time it takes to perform the necessary getting-ready tasks. When proper training methods are utilized, children should, and can, learn their own timetables.

Engaging in battles about being ready not only takes the responsibility for being on time away from the child but also creates problems in the relationship between the parent and the child. Parents must learn alternate methods of handling the problem.

> Mr. and Mrs. K. constantly yelled, pleaded, and threatened ten-year-old Joan. Despite their efforts, they were almost always late, which often caused them some embarrassment when they were due at a friend's house for dinner.
>
> Mr. and Mrs. K. had also tried starting to get Joan ready well in advance of the scheduled time to leave. Joan constantly dawdled in the shower and took the longest time to get dressed. Regardless of when they "turned on Joan's motor," her running speed was always the same—slow!

Joan has discovered that she can control, frustrate, and embarrass her parents through her dawdling behavior. She defeats their every attempt to "make" her hurry up. Mr. and Mrs. K. fail to see that there is no way that they can *force* Joan to be ready on time.

But Mr. and Mrs. K. can gain Joan's cooperation by changing their approach. First of all, they must ask Joan before each occasion whether or not she wishes to accompany them. If Joan indicates that she does not wish to accompany her parents on a certain outing, her wishes should be respected. Children often resent being forced to go with their parents each time the parents decide that they wish to have the children with them. It is important to respect the child's desires if parents wish to gain cooperation when they absolutely must take the child—for example, when they are given short notice and are unable to get a baby-sitter.

If Joan says that she wants to go, then the parents should prearrange for a baby-sitter just in case she is not ready on time.

Let's suppose this happened.

> One evening, at a reasonable time before leaving, Mr. K. approached Joan. "Joan, we'll be leaving at seven o'clock. If you wish to come with us, you will have to be ready at that time. If you are not ready, Audrey will come to sit."
>
> Mr. and Mrs. K. refrained from further comment. At six forty-five Joan was still not ready, and it was apparent that she would not be able to get cleaned up and dressed in time. Therefore Mr. K. called the sitter.
>
> At seven the doorbell rang, and Mrs. K. let Audrey in. Joan began to realize what was about to take place. She ran to her mother and father, who were ready to leave.
>
> "Mom, Dad, just a few more minutes, I'll rush, please don't go," cried Joan.
>
> "I know you're upset, but it's seven o'clock and we have to leave. We'll see you when we get home." The parents left despite further pleas from Joan.

Mr. and Mrs. K. informed Joan what would take place if she were not ready on time, and they left the decision to her. Her behavior showed that Joan was not willing to be ready on time. Mr. and Mrs. K. refused to create a battleground by nagging and coaxing. They allowed Joan to take the consequences of her behavior. After one or two times of being left behind, Joan will probably learn to be ready.

PART III

THE CHILD
AT SCHOOL

CHAPTER 9

Approaches to Problems at School

PARENT-CHILD RELATIONSHIPS
CONCERNING SCHOOL

"James, I want to talk to you," said Mother. "I had a conference with your teacher today, and she said that if you do not start turning in your homework and stop fooling around in class, you are going to get F's on your report card. Now, I want you to get down to business, or I will take away all of your privileges. I'm going to talk to your teacher in a couple of weeks, and I'd better get a good report. Do you understand?"

This is a typical example of what happens in many homes when parents become frustrated with a child's lack of interest in school. Most parents believe they are doing what is best for the child by making sure he does his schoolwork. They feel that the child must take an interest in his studies in order to go to college, get a good job, assume responsibility. While these may be noble aspirations, we might question whether the parent is really motivated by them. Most parents feel proud of a child who achieves in school and ashamed of one who does not; their own abilities and their value as parents are threatened by a poor achiever. These parents often try to satisfy their own needs through a child's achievement.

Parents tend to ignore the most essential ingredient in any

child's development—the child himself. When the parent realizes that he is not entirely responsible for a child's school problems, or any other problems, a great burden is removed from the parent's shoulders and he is free to assist his child in ways that will help him mature. School is the child's problem, not his parents'. As long as the parent feels that his image is at stake, he will not be able to place the responsibility for school situations where it belongs.

For as long as Kay had been in school Mrs. Q. had diligently tutored her daughter at home. But despite Mother's efforts, Kay was not a good student and constantly struggled against attending the daily tutoring sessions.

During a parent group meeting Mrs. Q. gained a new perception of Kay's school grades. She realized that by working with Kay at home she was preventing her daughter from experiencing the necessity of becoming responsible for her own education. Mrs. Q. was skeptical about these ideas until one of the members asked her if she wanted her daughter to attend college some day. When Mrs. Q. replied that she hoped Kay would, the member asked if Mrs. Q. intended to go with her daughter to college. Then Mrs. Q. began to realize that this was the time to start helping her daughter learn responsibility.

That evening, after supper, Mrs. Q. approached her daughter. "Kay, for a long time I have worked with you and kept after you about your schoolwork. I have decided that there is no way I can make you learn. From now on, school is your job. You will have to decide what you are going to do about it." Kay looked very surprised at her mother's remarks.

Mrs. Q. has taken a big step toward helping her daughter assume responsibility. From the description of the interaction between Mrs. Q. and Kay during the tutoring sessions, it seems that by creating a struggle Kay was telling Mother, "You can't make me learn." The more the parent worries about a child's education, the more he tends to pressure the child and to create a battleground over schoolwork and achievement. The

child who is discouraged and rebellious will often use schoolwork as a weapon to defeat his parents. When the parent ad-
mits defeat and refuses to fight over school, as Mrs. Q. has done,
the child's weapon is useless. There is no payoff from not learning.

The parent must be firm in his decision not to interfere. The
child will test his parent to see if he really means what he says.
Most children who are told that schoolwork is their own responsibility will begin by doing nothing. When the parent
discovers this, he may be tempted to kindle the battle fires
again. This is exactly what the child expects. He feels certain
that the parent eventually will return to his old habits. If the
parent does fall back on force, he proves that the child was
correct in his assumption.

> One evening Jerry brought his social-studies book home and
> left it in the family room. When Mr. O. came home he
> noticed the book, but he did not mention it. While Dad was
> reading the newspaper Jerry said, "I've got a social-studies
> test tomorrow." Dad refrained from comment. Then Jerry
> stated, "But I'm not going to study for it." Again receiving
> no reply, Jerry said, "Aren't you going to say anything about
> this? Don't you care about my schoolwork?" Dad looked up.
> "It seems to me that you feel I should force you, but it is
> really your problem," he said. "I hope you do well, but you
> must decide." At this point Jerry dropped the conversation.

Here Dad has successfully stayed out of Jerry's trap. Dad
continued to place the responsibility in Jerry's lap by showing
Jerry what he was attempting to do and that it would not
work. He avoided lecturing and preaching comments such as
"Well, you'll have to take the consequences," "You're the one
who will suffer," "Go ahead and flunk if you want to."

Jerry may test Dad again, but if Dad remains firm and maintains his resolve, Jerry may decide to accept his responsibility.

Some parents help their children with their schoolwork
without battling. The child seems to learn as long as the parent

is working with him; however, he still does not achieve well in school. When teachers are asked about the child, they also report that he does well when they work individually with him, but there is little carry-over to his independent work. It is obvious that this child, and others like him, use schoolwork as an attention-getting device. Chances are they are often quite dependent in other ways as well. Again, if the parent is to help his child achieve independence and accept responsibility, he must shift the job of school to the child and at the same time find other ways to fulfill the child's desire for attention, through recognizing useful contributions.

For several nights six-year-old Patty brought home an arithmetic paper on which she had missed nine out of ten problems. Each night her father patiently went over each error with his daughter. Even though Patty seemed to grasp the concepts after each tutoring session, she still would miss the same number of problems. Her father then would go over the errors with her again.

A parent study group helped Father to see that Patty, who was dependent in many other areas, apparently used mistakes to gain his attention and service.

When Father returned home from work the following day he found Patty sitting on the couch in the living room with her usual paper in hand. "Hi, Patty," he said, and went into the family room to read his evening newspaper. In a few minutes Patty entered the family room, still holding her paper. Father again said, "Hi," and continued reading. Patty carefully removed everything from the coffee table and laid her paper right in the middle. At this point Father retired to the bedroom, announcing that he was going to take a nap. A short time later he was called to dinner. When he arrived at the table he discovered Patty's work sheet resting on his dinner plate. Unable to avoid some kind of comment, Father picked up the paper and declared, smiling, "Oh, I see you got one right," and handed the paper back to Patty.

The next evening when Father came home he again found Patty sitting on the living room couch. Before he could get out to the family room, she ran up to him, holding her paper out to him and stating, "Daddy, I got all of them right." Father smiled and replied, "I knew you could do it!"

This factual incident illustrates how a parent can render futile a child's efforts to gain attention by focusing on work that is correct rather than on errors. Through Father's action Patty discovered that she could no longer gain attention by making mistakes. If she wanted Father's attention she would have to concentrate her efforts on getting problems right rather than wrong.

In addition to grades and homework, the child must learn to accept the responsibility for all school situations. For instance, each child must learn to deal with each teacher he encounters. Sometimes parents will mistakenly assume the responsiblity for their child's discipline at school.

> Johnny, age ten, enters the house after school. Mother meets him with an angry look on her face. "Your teacher called me today and said that you never stay in your seat and are continually talking out and disturbing the class." Johnny replies, "She's just mean. She never—" Mother sternly states, "I don't care what you think of Miss J. You had better stay in your seat and be quiet! I don't want to hear a report like this again. Go to your room and think about what I said."

After an unpleasant report from the teacher, an incident such as this is not uncommon. Many mothers attempt to make their children behave properly in school by lecturing, threatening, and punishing. It is obvious that the teacher has a poor relationship with Johnny; why should Mother compound the problem by impairing her own relationship with him? If Mother feels Johnny's behavior in school is a reflection on herself as a mother, then it is easy to understand why she behaves in this way. But if Mother did not feel responsible for Johnny's behavior, she could place the responsibility for the problem where it belongs, between Johnny and his teacher.

In fact, if Mother had not felt responsible for Johnny's behavior, the incident probably never would have occurred. The phone conversation might have proceeded like this:

MISS J.: Hello, Mrs. N., this is Miss J., Johnny's teacher. I called to inform you that I am having problems with Johnny. He won't stay in his seat, and keeps talking out of turn and disturbing the class.

MRS. N.: I can see that it would be difficult to teach with this going on.

MISS J.: Yes, it is. Would you please speak to him when he gets home this evening?

MRS. N.: I would, Miss J., but this has happened before, and my speaking to him never improved the situation. If I scold him at home he sometimes tries to get even with the teacher, so I'd rather not.

MISS J.: Then I really don't know what to do.

MRS. N.: I'm sure he can be very difficult, but I'm confident that you'll be able to take care of the situation.

Mother sympathized with the teacher, but she did not assume responsibility for Johnny's behavior by responding to the teacher's request. Instead, she has given the teacher her permission to deal with the problem as she sees fit. If the teacher is open to suggestions, as this teacher seemed to be, and the mother feels that she could make a helpful suggestion, then it would be appropriate for her to do so. If, on the other hand, she did not have a suggestion, she should do as this mother did.

Sometimes children are sent home from school because of their behavior. When this happens many parents become unduly upset and make the situation worse. Most children would rather be in school than stay home, because, even if they dislike it, school is where their friends are. Staying home may be exciting at first, but after a while the novelty is gone. However, if the child is rewarded by stirring up a lot of commotion and concern within the family, he may be willing to accept the unpleasantness in order to get the reward.

The problem of the child's school behavior is really between the child and the school. The parent must avoid creating a parent-child problem. The child has already experienced the consequence of his misbehavior. Additional consequences, such as sending him to his room or banning television, will be interpreted as punishment. Remaining calm and allowing the child to find ways to occupy his time will be much more effective.

SCHOOL PROPERTY

Occasionally the parent may face the problem of the child's irresponsible use of school materials or property. In most cases the school informs the parent that he is expected to pay for or replace a damaged or lost article. Many parents make the mistake of becoming angry with the child while at the same time assuming his responsibility by paying for the materials. In order to train the child to be responsible for materials loaned to him, alternative approaches need to be considered.

> Mrs. P. was told in a phone call from the school principal that her son, Ricky, had become angry at school and had torn one of his textbooks. He explained that the damaged book would have to be paid for.

If Mrs. P. is going to help her son learn that he must be responsible for materials not belonging to him, there are basically two avenues of action open to her: (1) She can completely remove herself by informing the principal that she feels he and Ricky should work out the problem to the principal's satisfaction; for example, he could have Ricky pay for the article out of his allowance each week. (2) She can pay for the book and have Ricky reimburse her.

If the parent decides to pay for a lost or damaged article and require the child to make restitution, he should offer the child a choice of how he wishes to repay him. Perhaps the child may be offered the alternatives of paying for it out of his allowance or doing extra jobs. Choice in every instance is a most powerful tool, since it respects the child's capacity to decide, makes him responsible for his behavior, and generally elicits his cooperation. Sometimes, however, the child may say "I don't know" when given a choice. In this case the parent should ask him to think about the matter and be ready with an answer by a certain time. If the child still refuses to choose, then the parent will have to make the decision. It is advisable that the parent decide to collect the money from the child's allowance, as making sure he does extra jobs may present further difficulties.

PARENT-TEACHER RELATIONSHIPS

In school corridors, in the teachers' lounge, and in discussions among school personnel, there appears to be a tendency to blame and accuse parents of causing their children's problems, not doing what the school considers best for their children, or interfering with what the school is trying to accomplish. In neighborhoods, local bridge clubs, across cups of coffee, at the supermarket, teachers and other school officials are often blamed, accused, and criticized for the methods or materials that they use is dealing with their students. In short, there seems to be a mutual lack of understanding and trust between schools and parents. Although there are certainly mistakes made on both sides, many conflicts could be resolved and attitudes changed through better communication. Sometimes teachers are not made aware of particular problems in the home that may be contributing to a particular child's difficulty in adjusting to the school situation. Similarly, parents are not always made aware of what the school is trying to do.

One way teachers try to facilitate communication to parents is by sending notes home. Unfortunately, this type of communication is usually of a negative nature.

Dear Mrs. B.,

I am writing to inform you that Amy is not completing her work in class. Furthermore, she is constantly bothering the other children. Please discuss her behavior with her.

Sincerely,
Miss Y.

It is quite possible that Mrs. B. has received notes such as this previously. Many teachers, out of desperation, attempt to discharge their responsibility by insisting that parents assume responsibility for teaching the child. How should Mrs. B. handle this situation? She should introduce the problem to Amy, not by lecturing or punishing, but by making an attempt to understand her feelings. Then together they can discuss solutions to the problem.

MOTHER: Amy, I would like to discuss this note with you. [Mother shows Amy the note and lets her read it.] It appears that you are not happy in school.

AMY: Miss Y. is mean, and the kids pick on me.

MOTHER: It seems as though nothing goes right for you in school. [Amy nods her head.] It must be *very* unpleasant for you to go to school each day.

AMY (sighs): It sure is.

MOTHER: Would you like to talk about it? Is there any way I can help out?

AMY: You could go tell that teacher to quit being so mean.

MOTHER: You'd really like me to straighten out that teacher.

AMY: Yes—will you?

MOTHER: I'm sorry, Amy, but I don't feel that is my responsibility; this is between you and your teacher. But I'll be glad to help you decide what you can do about it. Would you like to do that?

Here Mother has used reflective listening to demonstrate her acceptance of Amy's feeling. She has been empathetic while remaining firm in her own feeling that the responsibility for handling the situation really belongs to Amy. She has conveyed her feelings to Amy by using an "I Message," and she has offered to assist in exploring alternatives. If Amy appears unwilling to discuss what she could do, Mother should not push, but instead recognize her feelings and remain available: "I see you would rather not talk about what you might do right now. If you change your mind, let me know, and I'll try to help."

After discussion with Amy, Mrs. B. could reply to the note in some such way:

> Dear Miss Y.,
> We were interested to learn about your concern, and we have discussed the problem with Amy. We believe it is up to Amy to take care of this—we are sure she can do it.
> Sincerely,
Mr. & Mrs. B.

If the teacher insists on trying to involve the parents in discipline or supervision of school-related problems which the parents believe are in opposition to their philosophy of parent-child relations, then it will be important to arrange a conference with the principal to discuss, in a friendly manner, the parents' rationale and philosophy and a possible change of teachers. Just as we might change our doctor or lawyer because of a difference in philosophy or values, we can also change teachers; we cannot expect a teacher to be able to deal with all children. This is not to be interpreted as a reflection on the capabilities of the teacher, but really as a recognition of individual differences.

Another attempt at communication is the parent-teacher conference. Let us eavesdrop on a typical meeting.

> TEACHER (after usual social amenities): Larry is having some difficulties in school this year.
> MOTHER: What seems to be the problem?
> TEACHER: He doesn't seem to be working up to capacity. His aptitude scores show he could do much better than he is actually doing.

MOTHER: Yes, I am sure you're right. Last year his teacher said the same thing.

TEACHER: He's a likable boy, but many times he fools around instead of working, and I have to keep after him to finish his assignments.

MOTHER: Why do you think he is having these problems?

TEACHER: I would say he's immature.

MOTHER: Yes, we notice that at home too. Is there anything you could suggest we could do to help Larry?

TEACHER: Since he is immature, he doesn't seem able to work on his own, and apparently requires pushing. He has to learn to be responsible for getting his schoolwork done, and he must develop good work habits. If I could send some work home, and if you would sit with him each night and make sure he does it, I think that might help. What do you think?

MOTHER: Yes, I think you're right. I'd be willing to do that.

Let's see what went on in this typical parent-teacher conference. First of all, both teacher and mother agree that Larry has a problem. Second, both agree on what they consider to be the "cause" of the problem. Third, they are in agreement about what Larry needs to learn. Fourth, they agree on what needs to be done. And fifth, neither one really understands the child or knows what to do with him! This is not a criticism of either the teacher or the parent, but of their child-relationship skills.

To label a child "immature" does not facilitate understanding. This definition of maturity is so nebulous that it is doubtful that anyone could be considered "mature." Both teacher and parent must understand the movement of the child. It appears from the comments concerning the "need" to be pushed that Larry desires to show his power. He proves that "no one can make me learn!"

Both mother and teacher are correct when they say that Larry must become responsible for his schoolwork. But "making" him does not help him develop responsibility. Instead, it takes it from him. Both parent and teacher must *give* Larry the responsibility for learning if they expect him to accept it. In other words, instead of pushing him, they should do just the opposite. Trying to force a child who wants to show his power only reinforces his goal.

Both the teacher and the parent are making a mistake in terms of influencing Larry by collaborating on what to do about his lessons. The teacher should not expect the parent to assume the responsibility for teaching Larry, nor should the mother accept it. As mentioned previously in this chapter, if the child is going to become responsible for his education, the parents must refrain from taking the responsibility away from him. Mother *can* help by giving Larry responsibilities at home. In this way she can win his cooperation and facilitate self-discipline and motivation.

Unfortunately, many parent-teacher conferences are not as helpful as they could be. Teachers need to develop more understanding of children and more practical suggestions for parents.

Sometimes it is the parent who has the complaint. This situation often causes hostile feelings between the parent and the teacher. Some parents persist in dressing down teachers when they feel their child had been wronged. Obviously, this type of approach will seldom produce cooperation. Other parents automatically call the principal when a problem arises. Some call the superintendent. Going over the teacher's or principal's head also can promote negative feelings. In addition, none of the above methods benefit the child in the end. Following are a few suggestions for procedures that have been found helpful when a problem arises at school.

1. Find out the facts and the feelings: When your child tells you something that you feel needs further attention, call the teacher first and ask him about it.

2. Remain friendly and keep an open mind: Remember, regardless of how you feel about his philosophy or action, you should listen to what the teacher is saying, indicate that you understand his position, and hear him out before interpreting.

3. Follow the chain of command: As suggested in point 1, talk with the teacher first. If you do not gain satisfaction, then it is logical to talk with the principal. If still no satisfaction is derived, you may wish to talk with those having more authority.

Although teachers and other school personnel are quite used to receiving complaints, very few ever hear expressions of appreciation from parents. Teachers need encouragement too. Therefore it is very important to inform school people when things are going well. Let them know you appreciate what they are doing. Mention specific methods that you feel have helped. This type of communication is especially helpful with a teacher with whom you have had difficulty. A sincere word of encouragement goes a long way toward establishing more positive feelings. A short note expressing your feelings is sometimes very effective with a difficult teacher.

THE TEACHER AS A VICTIM OF THE PAST

Rapid social change has left many teachers unprepared to meet the challenges presented by today's children. They may have limited training in understanding child behavior or be unaware of practical approaches to misbehavior and learning problems. Too often they find themselves relying on old, autocratic methods to solve problems that can have successful solutions only if handled democratically.

As a result, teachers become discouraged when faced with expectations they cannot possibly fulfill. They often feel responsible for each child's behavior and learning, and believe that they should be able to "make" each child learn and behave properly. They try desperately to find ways to get the child to perform—rewards, punishments, trying to get parents to apply pressure.

Many teachers are "good mothers" in the sense that they are

very concerned with their image: "A child I can't make learn or behave well makes me look like a bad teacher." This is an attitude that stems from an autocratic heritage—the leader is responsible for everyone's performance. This concept is no longer appropriate, and teachers, like parents, must learn to help children accept their own responsibilities. They must learn to function democratically.

THE MOVEMENT TOWARD HUMANIZATION OF THE SCHOOLS

Fortunately, many colleges are becoming aware of the need to provide teachers with practical methods applicable to their classroom experience. The University of Florida, as a result of the research and writing of Dr. Arthur Combs and others, has designed a program for humanizing education. The uniqueness of the approach derives from the fact that in addition to training teachers to utilize positive approaches to children, the teachers-in-training are valued as persons themselves, in the belief that they will learn more from what they experience than from what they are told (Blume, 1971).

In addition to a new awareness on the college level, individual school systems are taking steps to improve themselves. Individualized instruction, the open classroom, employment of special personnel—including counselors in the elementary school—and in-service training in human relationships are all attempts to humanize the educational experience for children.

Parents must realize that institutional change is slow, but they can be of help to their own school systems by implementing the suggestions discussed in the following section.

HOW PARENTS CAN HELP THEIR SCHOOLS

The official policy-making organization in any school district is the local board of education, whose board meetings are generally open to the public. Parents can become more involved in the events within their school district by attending board meetings, learning the nature of the issues being discussed, and discovering the attitudes of the board members. Although articles are published in school bulletins and local newspapers, attendance at board meetings may give parents a clearer picture of the board function.

In addition, almost every school in our country has a parent-teacher association. Although these organizations are beneficial, they are not often as helpful as they could be. The function of the PTA in many schools seems to be quite superficial, restricted basically to fund raising, and the attendance at meetings is rarely representative of the school parentage.

PTA can become a more influential organization by keeping abreast and informing its members of the policies and activities of the school. Many PTAs are moving in this direction by allowing school personnel to present information about the programs with which they are involved. The PTA has the potential to be a major facilitator of communication between the school and the community it serves. This can be accomplished by presenting more programs dealing with issues that are of major concern to both school and community, and by sponsoring parent groups to discuss problems with children.

It is the parents' responsibility to keep abreast of school matters. The school can make every effort to communicate with and involve parents, but if parents do not avail themselves of the avenues of communication and involvement, little can be accomplished.

REFERENCES

Blume, Robert. "Humanizing Teacher Education," *Phi Delta Kappan* (March 1971). Dayton, Ohio: United Color Press.

PART IV

TOWARD
A DEMOCRATIC
FAMILY

CHAPTER 10

The Family Meeting

Are your children part of the family? Recalling that "equal" refers only to worth and dignity, and not ability and responsibility, do your children have equal status with the adults in the family? Do you assign children chores and times to do them, or can they help in planning? Do you try to decide their recreational activities, study hours, and clothing? Do you treat them less considerately than your friends?

We believe that having a voice in family affairs promotes responsible behavior and self-discipline. Children should be allowed to participate in decisions that affect their lives. If you are going to develop new, effective, and democratic relationships in the family, you will need:

1. The time and opportunity to communicate your ideas.
2. Feedback and reactions from the members of the family.
3. The commitment to invest time in communicating and processing feedback on a regular basis.

Parents must decide on the type of relationships they hope to promote in the family. These relationships are very dependent on the model established by the leadership roles of the parents. Leadership roles can be classified as authoritarian, democratic, or *laissez-faire* in style. These styles differ in terms of very basic issues. The typical leader's role in each of these three styles can be depicted as follows:

Autocratic	Democratic	Laissez-Faire
Dominate and make all decisions.	Offer choice situations.	Avoid reaching formal decisions.
Allow little group initiative.	Encourage group initiative and planning.	Allow complete freedom.
Keep all responsibility.	Delegate responsibility.	Do not attempt to regulate.
Make and enforce rules.	Encourage the group to formulate guides for conduct.	Make or enforce no rules, resulting chaos.
Demand respect from members.	Encourage mutual respect for each other.	Be unconcerned with respect.

While parents are seldom completely democratic or completely autocratic, it is possible to note the prevailing characteristic leadership style. In the past, autocrats were fairly successful, if we accept control as a criterion for success. The general abandonment of the autocratic model in politics, society, and education has caused the autocrat to be less effective in the family. He is more often humored or pitied than obeyed. The autocrat who makes pronouncements is given full responsibility for enforcing them and receives no cooperation.

The original reaction to the autocratic style was the permissive approach, which avoids decisions and rules and does not lead to effective relationships. We have observed that when a child is raised only with self-interest, he readily becomes bored and unhappy.

The democratic approach has as its target the development of autonomous but interdependent individuals who are free to make choices in a socially responsible manner. The leader benefits from sharing ideas, receiving feedback, and delegating responsibility, and he engenders more cooperation while meeting less resistance.

The family meeting is one of the most effective procedures for instituting democratic procedures. It provides a regular opportunity for family members to communicate and listen to the reactions of others. New approaches and ideas can only be absorbed when they can be heard and discussed and when their relevance to specific situations is made clear. Establishing family meetings is a decision made by members of the family, usually parents—although we have observed that children talking to other children about the benefits of the meeting can be powerful salesmen. It is decided that in order to communicate more effectively it is necessary to meet regularly to discuss relationships, share ideas, and make plans.

Productive family meetings are not motivated by a desire to control through a new gimmick, nor are they convened primarily to establish control and set rules. They are motivated by the desire to improve relationships, share responsibilities, and truly enjoy each other as members of a family. They must be characterized by the desire to hear each other's feelings, beliefs, and values. They must be concerned with pointing out what is right and finding assets instead of decrying weakness and labeling liabilities. The meetings can provide a unique setting in which to reveal positive as well as negative feelings, where children learn to listen to each other, and parents have an opportunity to listen to the child's perception of his needs and place in the family.

The family meeting is not a magical solution to human relationships; it can be only as effective as the good intentions and listening skills of the participants. But it should provide a special opportunity to restore the human relationships within the family which the pace of modern living, television, and the mobile society have stolen from us.

PURPOSE OF MEETINGS

The family meeting is a regularly scheduled weekly meeting of all members of the family, planned for a mutually convenient time when all can attend. If certain family members choose not to attend, decisions still can be made which affect them. If they desire to change these decisions, it is their responsibility to appear at the next meeting.

The meeting takes into consideration all of the relationships and business affecting the family. A typical set of family meetings will include:

1. Opportunities to give information about coming events, plans for fun or work, changes in living arrangements, vacations: Family meetings might announce a weekend trip, the visit of a relative or special friend, the building or remodeling of housing facilities, and the implications of these events for living in the home. Progress by family members or progress on family concerns can be communicated. For example, members may announce progress made academically, athletically, musically, in clubs, or in neighborhood activities. The family meeting should be a time for sharing good news and mutual encouragement.

2. Plans and decisions: The child learns best when he is given the opportunity to plan, decide, and take responsibility for his judgment. The parent will secure cooperation most readily by allowing the child to participate in decision-making that affects him directly. Dialogue, discussion, and varied opinions and ideas are always more time-consuming, but plans and decisions are more satisfactory when they result from group thinking, increased involvement, and the cooperation of all family members. Participation in decision-making also helps develop self-assurance in the child.

3. An opportunity for dealing with recurring problems that cause conflict: In contrast to times of conflict, when family members are primarily concerned with winning their way and venting their emotions, the meeting should provide a chance to review the problem with perspective in a setting that is less crisis-oriented. While members may still have a high investment in winning or getting their way, their emotional tone will be lower than in the midst of conflicts, which will permit better relationships and more creative thinking. And the interven-

ing time between meetings often allows them to consider how others feel about the issue. Problems are not solved by anger, nagging, condemning, or avoidance, but through dialogue that enables members to reach agreement.

For example, Billy and Sue May want to watch different shows on television at 7:00 P.M. During the conflict it is difficult to reach a resolution that is mutually agreeable. But in the setting of the meeting, it may become obvious that they can easily alternate evenings, letting Sue choose the television show on Monday, Bill on Tuesday, and so on, or they could alternate weeks. One might even be able to persuade the other that the program he prefers would be best for both of them to view. The meeting provides the setting for looking at the issue, considering alternatives, and reaching satisfactory solutions.

4. An opportunity to discuss ways in which all may work together for the family good: In every family there are a variety of necessary tasks to be done involving food preparation, setting and clearing the table, washing dishes, disposing of garbage, cleaning the house, and running errands. The "good mother" often takes on all these responsibilities, depriving the children of the opportunity to learn skills, contribute to the family, and become independent. Children and parents should discuss the most effective way to share responsibilities, make decisions, and cooperate in accomplishing the tasks.

5. An opportunity to articulate concerns and complaints: Family living, by nature of its interrelationships and the proximity of members, produces tensions and disagreements. Poor communication and failure to state dissatisfactions with relationships, expectations, and responsibilities can provide daily irritation. At family meetings parents and children can come together to express their feelings and to make known things they would like to change.

Betty is always expected to wash dishes, but she would really like to get involved in the cooking instead. Mother feels that Betty resists helping. The opportunity to clarify produces understanding, more effective help, and most important of all, a relationship clearly signifying that Mother understands and that work is not a punishment.

Discussing differences of opinion at the weekly meeting can often eliminate continual bickering. If Kent and Teddy have come to an agreement about television that Kent refuses to live up to, there does not have to be a daily argument. If they are not yet responsible enough to keep their agreements, television can be discontinued until the next meeting. When there are complaints, they can sometimes be deferred for more effective action by requesting that they be brought up at the family meeting.

6. A social learning experience: The family is the original source of attitudes toward social living. The child develops his opinion of self and social relationships in this setting. If our goal is to produce independent but interdependent humans who care and are concerned about others, we may best be able to teach this through the interaction possible in the meeting. The child develops social interest, cooperation, the capacity to give and take, while the parents reap the benefit of improved relationships.

The meetings also help to create feelings of involvement in the family, conveying an attitude that the child's opinion is of value. The child feels accepted and develops a feeling of belonging, which strengthens his security.

INITIATING THE FAMILY MEETING

Meetings can begin after the parents have a clear understanding of the purpose of the meeting and its benefits, and have decided to develop democratic human relationships. Even benevolent tyrants will not survive the family meeting, so it is important to understand its present and long-term gains.

While it is best if both parents desire a family meeting, the meeting can also be conducted successfully by one parent if he believes in its philosophy and benefits. Even in situations where there is only one parent and only one child, it has been found that the regular opportunity for dialogue and discussion is beneficial, and age is no handicap as long as the child can communicate clearly.

Once the parents understand the philosophy and procedures of the family meeting, they meet with the children to explain the format of the meeting. The children are involved from the beginning by participating in decisions about the time of the meeting and the place. It is important to select a time when all members can attend and to avoid times when fatigue or pressures of appointments will handicap progress and jeopardize the human relationships.

GENERAL RULES

The chairman of the first meeting should be the member of the family who is most interested in developing democratic relationships and who is able to hear feelings, identify beliefs, and help members see each other's points of view while reaching agreement. The first chairman is usually one of the parents, but each week the chairmanship should rotate to another member of the family—perhaps passing to the other parent for the second meeting, and then from the oldest to the youngest child, finally returning to the original chairman. Even the child considered incapable of being chairman will learn from the example set in the first meetings.

The chairman's duties involve beginning and closing the meeting precisely at the prearranged times. A meeting usually lasts for an hour at the maximum. The chairman decides who has the floor, and he keeps order so that each speaker can be heard. He makes certain that all points of view are heard, and therefore frequently encourages others to speak before him. The chairman helps the group focus on the topic and the issue, and he does not permit a change of topics until there has been an opportunity for full discussion and some resolution of the concern.

The rules for the family meeting should be kept simple. The purpose is to expedite communication between members, not to teach formal meeting procedures. The following simple guidelines should be sufficient:

1. A member has the floor by being recognized by the chairman.

2. When a person has the floor and is presenting his ideas, members cannot talk.

3. It is a good practice to have other members of the family restate what was presented to improve listening skills.

4. Members who have the floor are asked to comment on the points or issue being discussed. They are not to start new topics unless the concern being discussed is resolved.

5. Family decisions can be made that influence members who choose not to attend. Attending members, however, should not plot to punish those not attending.

6. Calling an emergency meeting or cancelling a meeting requires the unanimous permission of all family members.

7. The goal of the meeting is communication and agreement on issues, policies, and relationships. When agreement cannot be reached, voting can be used as long as there is no attempt to impose the will of the majority on the minority and members have agreed in advance to settle deadlocks in this manner. It is usually best to reach decisions by consensus to avoid having a legalistic spirit invade the meetings.

8. The proceedings of the meeting should be kept in the form of minutes, which can be posted in several places, such as the children's rooms and the kitchen, depending on family preference.

Rules can be arranged to fit special needs of the family.

One of the purposes of the meeting is the distribution of tasks and chores. The distribution is best accomplished by having the parents and children together compile a list of jobs around the house: cooking, food preparation, setting the table, clearing the table, disposing of garbage, errands, dusting, vacuuming, washing, ironing, shopping, care of pets, repairs, outdoor jobs, washing car, care of personal belongings, and care of one's own room. After the list has been completed, the children can participate in deciding what services they can contribute for the welfare of the family. It is important to avoid assigning children jobs that no one else will accept, and to be certain that their participation is a real contribution. If there are some unpopular jobs, such as taking out the garbage, all should take turns performing the job.

The children also can participate in deciding on a fair way to distribute the jobs. Parents should try to elicit volunteers, and if necessary, they might begin by volunteering themselves for less desirable jobs. This will help create a spirit of good will and a feeling of equality. Some families have resolved the issue by having a job jar containing slips of paper describing all the jobs for the week and when they are to be accomplished. The family members then pick slips from the jar. Each member does the job described on the slip he has selected. Each week a new drawing is held.

PROCEDURES, AND THE FIRST MEETING

Choose an area where each member of the family can be comfortable. Encourage every person who lives in the house, including grandparents, to join the meeting. The chairman will open the meeting, and the secretary will record the minutes. The agenda might include:

1. Beginning with the second meeting, reading of the minutes of the previous meeting. This will be essentially a report on decisions previously made.

2. Old business, discussion of issues not resolved, or situations that members may feel need to be changed.

3. New business. This should usually include plans for some pleasant undertaking by the family, or family fun.

4. Paying of allowances of settling other financial transactions between parents and children.

5. At the end of the meeting a summary of the major points and decisions and clarifying commitments. After this the time for the next meeting is set.

The meeting should be characterized by a spirit of mutual respect and a concern for open discussion and honest dialogue, with an emphasis on resolution of conflict through democratic procedures. When agreements made in the meeting are broken, the person or persons responsible for the violation are subject to logical consequences. All agreements are in effect until the next meeting, at which time they can be renegotiated if necessary.

Since chores and allowance are two concerns usually regulated by the family meeting, we have chosen them in our sample family meeting, with further specific suggestions following.

EXAMPLE OF AN INITIAL
FAMILY MEETING

This family consists of four members: Mom, Dad, Rob, eleven, and Ralph, nine.

DAD: I thought we might start having regular family meetings where we could talk about how we feel about the way things are going in our family. If we have any problems, we could discuss them and make some decisions. What do you all think about this idea? Would you like to give this a try? (Family agrees to try.)

DAD: Good. First of all, I would like to ask if this time and place is convenient for everybody.

ROB: The time is okay, but I don't like sitting at this table.

DAD: How do the others feel?

RALPH: I agree with Rob.

MOM: This is fine with me, but if the rest of the family is not comfortable, I would be willing to move.

DAD: Then we'll move. Any suggestions?

RALPH: Why don't we go into the family room? It's comfortable in there.

DAD: Is that okay with everybody? (Family agrees; after moving, Dad continues.) I have written down three things: 1. Old business. 2. New business. 3. Paying of allowances. Under the old and new business items we can present our complaints and problems for discussion and try to reach some agreements and solutions that are acceptable to all of us. We don't want some people to get their way at the expense of others. Also under "new business" we could plan some family fun each week. How does that sound? (Family responds favorably.)

MOM: I guess first we might talk about rotating the chairmanship. (Family decides the order of chairmen.)

DAD: Okay, now that we have that settled, maybe we can discuss the ground rules. Mother, will you take the minutes? (Family agrees, and Dad tells family about members speaking one at a time, listening to each other, etc.)

DAD: Do we have any old business, any problems or complaints about the way things are going?

ROB: There are a lot of things I don't like. For instance, I don't like the job of taking the trash cans out and bringing them in. When both cars are in the garage, I'm afraid I'll scratch one of them. And it's too smelly and grubby. The puppy's papers are the sloppiest job of all.

DAD: In other words, you don't like to do unpleasant jobs.

ROB: That's right.

MOM: I have to be honest and say that I don't like unpleasant jobs either, like cleaning the bathroom. I can appreciate how Rob feels.

RALPH: Me too.

DAD: You're all not in favor of doing unpleasant jobs.

MOM: No, but unfortunately they have to be done.

DAD: I'm not a lover of unpleasant jobs myself. So we have four people who don't like to do unpleasant jobs, and we don't have a robot around to take out the trash and clean up after the dog. Who has some suggestions about what we might do?

RALPH: We could take turns doing them.

DAD: Maybe before we decide, we should ask if there are any other unpleasant jobs we really don't like to do.

ROB: The toilet—cleaning the bathrooms. I sympathize with Mother.

DAD: Are there any others?

RALPH: There are trash cans, toilets, and dog. I can't think of any others.

MOM: For me dirty dishes are an unpleasant job. So that makes trash, toilets, dog, and dishes.

ROB: Cleaning my room, especially under the bed, is unpleasant.

DAD: That's true, but who does the room belong to?

ROB: Me.

DAD: That's right, and Ralph's room belongs to him, and our room belongs to us, so we are responsible for our own rooms. But these other jobs belong to all of us. Ralph, you said we could take turns. How does everybody feel about this? (Family agrees.)

DAD: Has anybody got any suggestions about deciding how we could take turns?

ROB: We could take turns on different days.

DAD: Okay, why don't we brainstorm? Do you all know what brainstorming is?

ROB: Everybody thinks up ideas.

MOM: Right—say everything you can think of, no matter how crazy it sounds.

DAD: Let's just see if we can think of everything we can without stopping to say "I like that" or "I don't like that." After we think up some ideas, we can comment on them. What other ideas do we have?

ROB: One person could do one part of the jobs and another person the other part.

RALPH: We could each take some jobs for a week and then trade.

DAD: I have a suggestion called the job jar. It simply means that you would write all those jobs on slips of paper and put them into a jar, and everyone would draw them out until they are all gone. Each person would do the job he drew for that week, and then at next week's meeting we would draw again. Are there any more suggestions? (Family indicates no.)

DAD: Why don't we go back over all the suggestions we have made so far and decide what we're going to do?

MOM: The first one was trade by days.

RALPH: I don't like that one.

MOM: The next one was splitting the jobs up into parts.

ROB: I like that one.

RALPH: So do I, because that way no one gets stuck with the whole awful job.

DAD: I don't care one way or the other, but it seems to me to be a little complicated. It would involve a lot of record keeping.

MOM: I don't feel this is a problem. For instance, one person empties the wastebaskets, the second takes the garbage cans out to the curb, and the third person brings them in. What's complicated about that?

ROB: A week is more complicated. It's really, really unpleasant doing these jobs for a whole week.

DAD: You mean you would prefer to have only part of the job, so that you wouldn't be stuck with it for a whole week. How about the rest of the family?

ROB: I kind of like the idea of splitting it up. I don't care for the idea of the whole week on one job.

RALPH: Me too.

DAD: Well, my only feeling about the whole week was that it was simpler, but if all of you are opposed, I'm willing to forget it. One thing that appeals to me is this job jar, but we could still use it if we modified it by putting on the slips, "Dog papers Thursday morning" or "Trash cans inside Monday night." How do you feel about that?

MOM: Now, let me be sure I understand how this job jar

is going to work. Are we going to split the jobs up into parts? That way no one would get stuck with the whole unpleasant job.

ROB: That's what I suggested—splitting each job up into parts for each day.

DAD: Well, it seems to me that we have come down to two ideas: the job jar and just choosing parts for the day. Now, what does everyone want to do?

MOM: I thought we were talking about using the two together.

RALPH: I want the job jar—it sounds more fair.

ROB: I like that one too. It's sort of like a game.

MOM: I'm not happy with the job jar, because it's easier for me to know that I have certain jobs to do at certain times, but I'm willing to give it a try in order to reach a solution.

RALPH: Oh, Dad, what if we pick two jobs for the dog on the same night? Do we have to do them both?

DAD: This is the one problem I see with the job jar. I would like you all to consider the element of chance. It is possible that you could draw "Clean up for the dog" four days in one week, and the next week you might not draw it at all. You have to consider this as opposed to the idea of signing up and trading equally every week.

ROB: I'm willing to take a chance.

RALPH: So am I.

DAD: It seems to me that we have settled this one, is that right? (Family agrees.)

DAD: But we need to decide on what goes in the list. Such as outside trash, and inside trash, and so forth.

ROB: We already decided on that, Dad. Mom has the list.

DAD: That's right. Then all we have to do is copy the list and cut up the slips. (Mother prepares the slips for drawing while the discussion continues.)

DAD: Any other old business? No? Okay, any new business?

ROB: It looks as if we settled quite a few of our problems. How about that family fun you talked about?

DAD: Let's see how everyone else feels. Any other problems? No? Then, how about some entertainment? (Family decides on a movie.)

DAD: Is there any other new business?

MOM: Just one thing. This may be old business, but I would like to say that I feel the boys have really been helpful this last week in helping me to clean the basement. I really appreciate it.

DAD: I'd like to add that I like the way you boys did some thinking during our meeting today. Shall we pay the allowances and adjourn? (Meeting adjourned.)

CHORES, AND HOW THE FAMILY MEETING CAN HELP

Parents often complain that children will not assume responsibility for doing necessary household duties. But the parent will discover that cooperation is more readily forthcoming from the child who is given the opportunity to participate in deciding which task he must perform than from the child whose chore is arbitrarily assigned to him. Family meetings provide the child with an over-all view of what is to be done and give him the responsibility of helping to decide who is to do it. Once the child has been involved in selecting and agreeing to perform certain duties, it can be expected that he will fulfill his agreements.

If the child does not perform the duties to which he has agreed, logical consequences should be applied. The concern should be discussed at the next meeting to see if the child wants to do the same job, or if he wishes to make changes. If there is still no cooperation, the parents should continue using logical consequences.

A General Approach to Breaking Agreements

The following example shows how one father solved the problem of the breaking of agreements.

At a family meeting Mr. and Mrs. E. and their two children, Beth, ten, and Bart, nine, had discussed what jobs had to be done around the house. The two children agreed to take care of their rooms, and along with Mr. E., they agreed to help their mother, who was a full-time university student, with the cleaning each Saturday morning. It was not long before the children began to neglect their agreements.

At a following family meeting Mr. E. discussed the problem with the children. He told them that in his business he used contracts. He explained to them that contracts were like agreements, and in a contract both parties agreed to do certain things. If one of the parties neglected his agreement, then the other party was not held to his part of the bargain. He applied this to their family situation. If the children did not keep their agreements, then the parents were not bound to keep the agreements they had made with the children—such as taking them out on weekends, which was a normal occurrence in their family.

For a while the children kept their agreements. But later they began to neglect their duties again. The parents refrained from comment. That Saturday the children asked their parents if they were going to be taken to the movies as had been agreed. Mr. E. answered, "I'm sorry, but we do not feel like keeping our agreements; we'll see how we feel next weekend."

Mr. and Mrs. E. reported that they seldom had difficulty in the future.

Mr. E. approached the problem in a logical manner that made sense to the children. When the children again broke their agreements, the parents did not nag or coax, but let the consequences take place. They assured the children of another chance. (This action could backfire quite easily if the parents had used it in such a way as to get even with the children.)

At What Age Should Children Become Involved in Household Chores?

Many parents wonder at what age children should be expected to do certain chores. This often depends on the attitude of the parents. The parent who feels it is his responsibility to make life comfortable for the child expects very little from him and usually gets what he expects! On the other hand, the parent who is overzealous tends to expect too much from his child. He often resorts to force in an attempt to "make" the child responsible.

Normally, when a child reaches the age when he is an active member of the family, he should be able to contribute by taking care of his personal belongings. As he begins to mature, he will be able to assume other responsibilities. Parents can aid his development by enlisting his help in performing certain duties. Many times a three- or four-year-old will enjoy helping Mother set the table. Or he may like to help make his own bed and straighten up his room. It is important to capitalize on any indication of a desire to cooperate with chores. A parent's high standards could leave him with a child who is never "old enough" to cooperate.

ALLOWANCES

Essentially, the reasons for giving each child an allowance are: (1) so that he may share in the family income, and (2) in order for him to develop a conception of the value of money and budgeting. As soon as the child has financial needs for contributions, recreation, or treats, an allowance can be started. The child should be given enough money to cover actual needs plus a small amount for savings. The allowance then may be modified to fit new needs. By the time a child is in second or third grade he may be given enough money each week to cover the cost of his lunch if it is purchased, savings, consumable school supplies such as paper, pencils, and so on, and spending money.

The purpose and use of the allowance can be discussed at a family meeting. Amounts of spending money can be negotiated. Allowances can be paid at the conclusion of the family meeting.

At times children may become spendthrifts. If parents allow them to experience the consequences of free spending, much can be learned.

At a family meeting Mr. and Mrs. G. discussed an allowance with their eight-year-old son, Dick. The parents had been giving him a small amount of spending money for about a year, and had now decided to give him the responsibility for his lunches, school supplies, and savings as well. Mr. G. and Dick figured the amount necessary for lunch each week, for spending money, and then added an extra quarter for savings and school supplies. After a short time Dick began to take his lunch from home and use the allotted lunch money for entertainment. In the next family meeting Father approached Dick.

> FATHER: I notice you have started to take your lunch instead of buying it. If this is the case, then you won't need weekly lunch money.
>
> DICK: Yes, but sometimes I still like to buy it.
>
> FATHER: Okay. What do you think would be a fair way to work this out?
>
> DICK: Well, maybe I could buy it about three times a week, and if I don't use the money I'll return it.
>
> FATHER: Fine. I like that idea.

Some parents make allowances a battleground by insisting that the child use his allowance for specific purposes, such as savings and church donations. This insistence often defeats what they are trying to accomplish. The child who does not save will learn the value of saving when he experiences the consequences of indiscriminate spending. And the child who does not wish to give part of his allowance to a church is usually expressing a self-centered attitude, which is best dealt with by establishing a more cooperative relationship with the child through the use of democratic principles.

An allowance can become a battleground if it is used as a

reward or punishment for chores accomplished or neglected. It is our feeling that the allowance should have no specific connection with duties the child is expected to perform. Children have a right to share in the family responsibilities. But these are separate and distinct. Mother and Father do not get paid for the jobs they do around the house. Children who are paid for what they should be expected to do as contributing members of the family often develop distorted values concerning money and responsibilities. When allowances are used as punishments, the same distortion usually occurs. In other words, withdrawing money for not doing chores is the same as paying for doing expected jobs.

The family meeting has great potential for improving human relationships. While it requires time, effort, and involvement, it also improves relationships more effectively than any other single procedure. It has been our experience that families who do not have time for meetings do not have time to train their children or to be mutually concerned. The frequency of family meetings is often a barometer of the family atmosphere. If there are regular meetings, it is less likely that there will be major storms and hurricanes. It is vital that the parent take the time to understand and implement the family meeting. Democratic meetings can help suggestions move from the pages of a book into action in your family.

CHAPTER 11

A Parent's Confidence-Building Guide to Effective Problem-Solving

RETRAINING AND RETHINKING TAKE TIME— BE PATIENT!

Your beliefs about children and how to interact with them are the result of a series of experiences that, in many instances, go back to your own childhood. You were once a child and experienced authoritarian, democratic, or *laissez-faire* approaches. Your experiences as a child have an influence on your beliefs about parent-child relationships. You may be repeating the pattern that your parents applied to you, but more than likely, you have rejected some of the basic constructs that governed parent-child relationships in your youth, and you are training your child with methods exactly the opposite of your own experiences. If your parents were very strict, you may be quite permissive. If your parents were permissive, as a parent you may be strict. Consider *how* you came to hold your present beliefs and assumptions about child training. It is important to recognize that if you are going to develop a new relationship with your child, you will have to examine your own beliefs about human relationships and human behavior—and *this takes time.*

Once you have committed yourself to a new program that values democratic approaches in contrast to authoritarian or permissive ones, you will still need to have patience. Your child has experienced you as either too strict or too lenient. He has a set of expectations and anticipations regarding your parental behavior. And he will not change instantly just because you have decided to relate in a more effective manner. If his past behavior has been rewarding to him, then there is little need for him to change. For example, if you immediately do his bidding whenever he complains, or if you assume his responsibility when he fails to cooperate, there is little for him to gain by changing his behavior. In the period during which you are attempting to change your relationship, recognize that your history with the child will have some effect upon how readily he is retrained.

Being patient involves refusing to be pressured by the child, relatives, neighbors, or the community's expectations of how a "good" mother should respond. You will recall that the "good" mother is the antithesis of our parental goal in child training. The child is usually clever, and quickly able to identify your sensitive spots. Do not respond to: "All the other kids . . . ," "Jimmy is lucky; he has a good mother," "You don't love me," "I hate you," or any other tactic designed to force you to revert to your old procedures. The child is usually more persistent in training the parent than the parent is in training the child.

You must be prepared for neighbors and relatives who may tend to discourage your efforts. Statements such as "They're only children once," "He's your baby," "All children . . ." are all designed to weaken your commitment to improved relations and communication. If your goal truly is to help your child mature while developing a cooperative relationship, then you will not be easily dissuaded.

DEMOCRACY IN FAMILY RELATIONSHIPS

The first task in achieving democratic relationships usually involves assessing the current relationships. This may make you aware of the way in which members may dominate each other in an authoritarian manner. In some instances the parent dominates, but more frequently we see that the child is really in control, forcing others to react to him. The task is to eliminate the superior-inferior relationships that currently exist in the family.

Conflict is frequently produced by family members who feel that they are better than others. If Father feels that he is the exception to all the rules and superior to Mother and the children, then there will be little opportunity for cooperation and the development of a democratic family. The same faulty relationships can exist between the dominant mother and the weak father, or the older child, who may feel he has more rights than the younger siblings. Family members who are treated as inferiors are always aware of their status, and this serves to interfere with new relationships. However, even if your spouse does not cooperate, *you* can still change *your* relationship with your children. The democratic approach requires that we place our belief about human beings into action in the primary atmosphere for learning—the family. It places a premium on the utilization of communication skills, encouragement, and logical consequences to facilitate the democratic experience. The power of positive parenthood opens the channels for two-way communication and willing cooperation.

THE COURAGE TO BE IMPERFECT

Our success with children often depends on our own standards and expectations. We have suggested that children need to be encouraged and that they should not be involved in pursuing perfection. It is only consistent to suggest that we are not interested in developing the "perfect parent." In reading this book, one will recognize that there are many situations in which as a parent you will continue to have difficulties. None can master all of the ideas. You cannot change your feelings and your behavior to the extent that you no longer have relationship problems with your child. The illusion that one can become the perfect parent must be dispelled. We might even go further and suggest that even if you could become such a paragon of virtue, it would not be good for the child. Perfect relationships at home would leave him unprepared to deal with all the faulty relationships in the real world.

If the parent is going to provide a model for human relationships, he must have a sense of his own personal strength and worth. He must not view his every mistake as a failure. In contrast, he must be able to see his own progress and not be pessimistic if changes do not occur immediately.

The courageous parent will not believe that the child's mistakes and faulty behavior are a personal attack or an insult to his strength or prestige. He will come to recognize that even though he has a most sincere commitment to a new approach and expends great effort, he will not be able to overcome all of the difficulties with the child. But it is essential that the parent has the courage to deal with his own imperfections and the desire to change old habits. This courage serves as a catalyst for the development of new human relationships. The target is not perfection, then, but developing the ability to cope effectively with the challenges of parent-child relationships.

BE MORE ACCEPTING OF YOURSELF

We have stressed the importance of accepting the child. But the child will not get this message unless the parent is able to accept himself. That is why we have also encouraged the parent to become more accepting of his own behavior. Many parents who feel extremely dissatisfied with their children are really, basically, dissatisfied with themselves. We are suggesting that the parent must become fulfilled as an adult, so that he doesn't require that his child serve as a symbol of his success or a buffer for his frustrations. For many parents their children have become symbols of their status in the community. The parent must not depend on the child to represent his own self and self-esteem. The child is from the parent and of the parent, but he is not the same as the parent. He is a separate being with unique needs, goals, values, and attitudes. The parent should involve himself in work and recreational and social relationships that produce the satisfaction he may have formerly sought from producing the perfect child.

FEELING GUILTY

Many parents report that they feel very guilty about the way in which they deal with their children. They say, "I know I am not doing things right; I'm too strict or too lenient, and I feel very guilty." We would like to emphasize that feeling guilty is often a cover-up. It is a suggestion of good intentions that we do not really have. We often observe people who feel guilty about such things as smoking, drinking, and poor communication with their spouse, but do nothing to improve or correct the situation. It is almost as if their expression of guilt makes them acceptable as good persons with good intentions, regardless of the fact that they really do not intend to change.

Sometimes parents play games with themselves when they recognize that their relationship with their child is unsatisfactory. They believe that the open acknowledgment of their guilt is sufficient. Supposedly their expressed good intentions should excuse their poor performance. But the expression of guilt does not solve the problem. If you want to change, make use of your capacity to decide and start to function in a more satisfying manner.

AVOID SELF-DEFEATING PATTERNS
OF BEHAVIOR

Parents are handicapped by a number of basic self-defeating patterns that are often the result of their faulty ideas about themselves and human relationships. We suggest that you look closely at some of the faulty assumptions that may cause poor relationships with your child (Ellis, 1962):

1. It is necessary to be loved or approved of by everyone in the community.

2. One must be thoroughly competent in all aspects of child training if he is to be considered personally worthwhile.

3. It is catastrophic when things do not turn out the way one would like.

4. Disobedience is a personal challenge to one's strength as a good parent.

5. We can do little about our problems, and we are the victims of circumstances.

6. The child's history determines his present behavior, and there is little that we can do to bring about a change.

7. The parent is completely responsible for the child's misbehavior, and since the child is only a product of the relationship, the child would not misbehave if the parent were a more effective person.

All of these mistaken ideas produce poor human relationships. They make the parent feel that he is "not OK." The parent must first change his beliefs, perceptions, actions, and attitudes before he can develop new relationships. These self-defeating patterns do not have to be repeated. The parent must choose to change.

AVOID DISCOURAGEMENT—BE POSITIVE

Throughout the book we have not only emphasized the debilitating effects of discouragement on the child but also cautioned the parent to have courage. As he develops his own personal philosophy of child training and examines his faulty assumptions about human relationships, he will recognize that he can change his own behavior and hence his relationship with the child. He can begin by making small but definite, positive steps. He must accept his efforts and not feel guilty about or discouraged by his mistakes. We have suggested that the parent regularly assess the positive qualities his child possesses. In addition, the parent should do this for himself. When he begins to get discouraged, he should focus on his accomplishments rather than on his failures.

The parent who is person-centered is aware of the child's feelings as well as his own. He shows his love and affection spontaneously and at unexpected moments, and through a physical contact he may communicate "I really think you're wonderful." He does not wait for the child to produce, and then acknowledge that "The B on the report card is very good." A person-centered parent is skilled at recognizing strengths and assets, and he is encouraging to the child.

The parent who is skilled at encouraging the child by recognizing his assets and strengths also will reflect and be able to recognize his own progress. This positive outlook, and the personal satisfaction gained from new relationships with the child and other members of the family, sustains his behavior. New relationships to produce new generations are a product of courageous parents who believe in themselves and their children.

PUTTING YOUR NEW SKILLS TO WORK

Now that you are resolutely committed to retraining yourself and to developing democratic relationships with your children, let us help you. We have compiled a series of self-tests and guides that will show you your progress and identify those areas that still present difficulties. Remember, you are not working for a perfect score or perfect relationships. But with courage, patience, and the consistent use of the democratic procedures described in this book, you will discover definite improvements in your family relationships.

These tests and guides will help you keep an eye on the positive results that are sure to follow. They will also serve as a quick and handy review of all the important democratic principles discussed in the book. Eventually you will not need to refer to the guides. Your new attitudes, beliefs, and responses will become a way of life, and the cooperation and growth of each family member will be more conclusive than the results of our self-tests.

But for now, when discouragement or impatience seems to be sneaking up on you, or when you feel a little baffled, we offer the following aids:

PRINCIPLES FOR DEMOCRATIC LIVING
WITH CHILDREN

Principle	Chapters
Understand the child's goals and behavior.	1
Recognize the power of expectations.	1, 5
Be both firm and kind.	1, 6
Understand the child's emotions.	2
De-emphasize competition.	2
Overlook mistakes.	2, 5
Don't be a "good" mother.	3
Accept the child *as he is.*	3, 5

Principle	Chapters
Become more consistent in your actions.	3
Separate the deed from the doer.	3, 5
Respect the child.	3
Encourage independence.	3
Avoid pity.	3
Be courageous and committed.	3
Refuse to be overconcerned about what others think.	3
Don't reinforce "getting."	3
Utilize listening skills.	3, 4
Recognize who owns the problem.	4
Use "I Messages" to send your feelings.	4
Restrict talking to friendly conversation.	4, 6
Watch your tone of voice.	4, 6
Don't "shout with your mouth shut."	4, 6
Refuse to fight or give in.	4
Withdraw from conflict.	4
Utilize problem-solving skills.	4
Apply natural and logical consequences.	4, 6, 7, 8, 9, 10
Select the appropriate approach.	4
Be creative—act, don't react.	4
Remember, rules are made for parents too.	4
Listen; children have good ideas.	4
Keep your control.	4
Have the courage to be imperfect.	4, 6, 11
Encourage the child.	5
Avoid performing tasks a child can do for himself.	6
Allow time for training.	6
Ask—don't demand.	6
Use correct timing.	6
Avoid involvement in children's fights.	7, 8
Don't play detective.	8
Treat the situation, not the offender.	8
School is the child's responsibility.	9
Hold regular family meetings.	10

Even though you become familiar with the principles, you may at times experience difficulties. Do not become discouraged. Remember that learning a new approach requires patience and practice. When problems develop, you may find the following suggestions helpful.

1. *Identifying the Child's Goal*

Always keep in mind the importance of identifying the child's goal. Remember, all children desire to belong. In any problem you encounter with your child, try to determine how he finds his place. Does he seek attention, power, revenge, or does he display inadequacy?

Here is a review of how to determine the child's goal. Keep in mind that the child may pursue his goal either actively or passively (except in goal 4).

Goal	Parent's Feeling and Action	Child's Reaction to Parent's Attempts to Correct Him
1. Attention	Parent is annoyed; wants to remind and coax.	Stops misbehavior. May repeat later or do something else to seek attention.
2. Power	Parent is angry, feels defeated, threatened; tries to show child he can't get away with this.	Continues the misbehavior; stops momentarily and repeats; or does what he is told, but not to the parent's standards.
3. Revenge	Parent is hurt; wants to retaliate.	Hurts back either by intensifying the misbehavior or choosing another weapon.
4. Display of inadequacy	Parent feels like giving up, throwing up hands: "What can I do?"	Passively accepts whatever is done, but does not improve.

After you have identified the child's goal by asking, "How did I feel?" and "What was my child's response to my attempts to correct him?" plan a course of action.

Consider: Should I reflectively listen, send an "I Message," problem-solve, encourage, ignore the misbehavior, or use consequences? Or is a combination of approaches needed? If the latter, which approaches, and in what order should they be used?

If you have identified the goal and applied a new approach, but still do not obtain positive results, utilize the "Troubleshooting Guide" to determine the source of the difficulty.

2. *The Troubleshooting Guide*

Occasionally you may try a method specifically illustrated in this book and experience failure. When such failure occurs, carefully analyze the situation.

First, write down *exactly* what you did and how the child responded. Second, use the following checklist to guide your investigation. When you determine the source(s) of the difficulty, reread the section(s) describing the principle involved. Be sure to read the reference(s) completely as you may have misunderstood more than one aspect of the principle or principles.

GENERAL PRINCIPLES

Did I talk too much?

Did I "shout with my mouth shut"?

Did I choose the appropriate approach?

Did I assume ownership of the child's problem (either during a listening session or with a problem where the consequences would occur outside the parent-child relationship)?

Did I neglect to encourage positive behavior?

Did I spend some friendly time with my child?

Did my tone of voice imply respect for the child?

Was I consistent?

Did I remain firm as well as kind?

FOR PROBLEMS INVOLVING THE USE OF
COMMUNICATION SKILLS

Did I truly listen or was I just saying words?

Did I misuse reflective listening through trying to manipulate or criticize?

Did I enter into exploring alternatives too soon?

Did I overdo reflective listening and/or alternative explorations?

Did my "I Message" focus on my feelings, or did I actually send disguised "You Messages"?

Did I overdo "I Messages"?

Did I enter problem-solving with preconceived solutions?

Did I try to manipulate during the problem-solving session?

Did I take enough time to listen, explore alternatives, or problem-solve?

FOR PROBLEMS INVOLVING CONSEQUENCES

Was my logical consequence truly logical and related to the misbehavior?

Did I use the correct timing?

Did I try to control with consequences? Did I *truly* allow the child to choose and accept his choice?

Did I use a logical consequence in a situation where a natural consequence was more appropriate?

FOR PROBLEMS INVOLVING THE FAMILY MEETING

Did I violate agreements made in family meetings?

Did I violate any principles or procedures of the family meeting?

Although experience indicates many typical problem areas in parent-child relations, it is impossible to anticipate every problem a parent may encounter. Therefore, we have developed a guide which can be used when a problem is experienced which is not covered in this book.

3. The Problem-Analysis and Correction Guide

The following is a kind a summary of the entire encounter between yourself and your child. Use this when you want to clarify, examine, or view your progress.

Guide	Comments
1. The incident.	Describe exactly what the child did. You may wish to include the time and place.
2. My action.	Describe your feelings and exactly what you said and/or did.
3. My child's reaction.	Describe exactly how the child responded to what you did—facial expressions, words, actions.
4. My child's goal.	Make a guess based on your feelings and his reaction to your attempts to correct him.
5. What principles did I fail to consider?	If you have trouble here, see the list of principles and the "Troubleshooting Guide."
6. My plan for redirecting his goal. a. discouraging the unacceptable misbehavior b. encouraging acceptable behavior	Describe exactly what you plan to do to correct the misbehavior. Refer to sections on communication, encouragement, consequences, and the family meeting.
7. Results (after at least one week).	Describe exactly what happened as a result of your plan. If not satisfactory, analyze (see "Troubleshooting Guide") and try again.

START A PARENT STUDY GROUP

Any new approach is difficult to learn, especially if you have to work alone. You will find that you can receive maximum benefit from your efforts to change if you can study the new ways with other parents.

In some regions you may find a professional who is familiar and in agreement with this approach to child training. If you find such an individual, encourage him to start a study group based on *Raising a Responsible Child: Practical Steps to Successful Family Relationships*.

If such a person is not available, you still can form your own group. Parents who have the courage to begin such a group will usually find the experience rewarding. Success is more likely if you do not play the expert. Let the participants know that you are interested in sharing some ideas from a book that has been helpful to you. Let the book be the authority. The purpose of the group will be to study and try to apply the approaches presented in *Raising a Responsible Child: Practical Steps to Successful Family Relationships*.

You can get a group started by talking to neighbors, friends, PTAs, clubs, church groups, and so on. Explain that you have read about some new ways to deal with the problems you have with your children, that they have been helpful, and that you wonder if they would be interested in forming a group to study and learn to apply the new methods.

A study group should be small enough to permit maximum participation. *Raising a Responsible Child: Practical Steps to Successful Family Relationships* should be studied chapter by chapter in order. Jumping ahead will be confusing and is usually unproductive. Members may bring up and discuss problems pertinent to each chapter.

The person leading the group should be familiar with the contents of *Raising a Responsible Child: Practical Steps to Successful Family Relationships*, and he should bring his book to each meeting and encourage others to do the same so that references to pages can be made if a point needs to be checked.

The meetings should be kept informal. Having coffee available and sitting in a circle can help.

Outline for Meetings

To be beneficial, each session should have some direction. We offer an outline for chapter study based on fifteen weekly meetings, each lasting an hour and a half to two hours.

Meeting	Chapter Discussed	Activity	Homework
1	Foreword	1. Establish purpose of group and method of study. 2. Settle any organizational business. 3. Have group read Foreword silently and discuss.	Read Chapter 1, "Understanding Behavior and Misbehavior."
2	Chapter 1	1. Discuss chapter. Be certain group clearly understands concept of purposive behavior, four goals of misbehavior, and life style. 2. Ask parents for examples of misbehavior in their own children and practice diagnosing goal of child.	Read Chapter 2, "Understanding and Promoting Emotional Growth."
3	Chapter 2	1. Discuss chapter. Make certain members understand the purposive nature of emotions and skills needed to promote emotional growth. 2. Ask parents to share problems involving emotions of their children and discuss.	Read Chapter 3, "Mistaken Concepts of Adults and Children."

Meeting	Chapter Discussed	Activity	Homework
4	Chapter 3	1. Discuss chapter. Make sure members understand each mistaken concept. 2. Briefly introduce listening skills (outlined in Chapter 3).	1. Read Chapter 4, "Communication," pp. 65–72. 2. Practice reflective listening. 3. Encourage parents not to try alternative exploration at this time, as beginning too early impedes listening.
5	Chapter 4, pp. 65–72.	1. Discuss need for listening skills and make certain members understand how traditional roles block communication. 2. Ask parents to report their first attempts at reflective listening. Analyze any problems. Role-play their experiences. Practice reflective listening.	1. Practice reflective listening. 2. Again discourage parents from trying alternative exploration at this time.
6	Chapter 4, pp. 65–72.	1. Continue practicing reflective listening, using methods outlined in fifth meeting.	1. Read Chapter 4, pp. 72–90 (remainder of chapter). 2. Encourage parents to try "I Messages" and problem-solving.

Meeting	Chapter Discussed	Activity	Homework
7	Chapter 4, pp. 72–90 (remainder of chapter).	1. Discuss remainder of Chapter 4. 2. Be sure parents understand concepts of "I Messages" and problem-solving approaches. 3. Ask parents to share experiences; analyze and role-play. 4. Practice sending "I Messages" and problem-solving. 5. Discuss thoroughly section "Selecting Approaches."	1. Practice reflective listening, "I Messages," and problem-solving. 2. If situation arises and parents feel they are ready, encourage alternative exploration.
8	Chapter 4, pp. 72–90 (remainder of chapter).	1. Ask parents to relate experiences. Analyze and role-play. More practice.	1. Read Chapter 5, "Encouragement." 2. Apply principles of encouragement.
9	Chapter 5	1. Discuss chapter. 2. Make certain members understand difference between praise and encouragement. 3. Ask parents to share experiences; analyze and discuss.	1. Read Chapter 6, "Learning Respect for Order Through Experience and Consequences." 2. Encourage parents to try out one or two consequences suggested that are related to problems they are having.
10	Chapter 6	1. Discuss chapter. 2. Make certain parents understand the concept of consequences. 3. Have participants share	1. Read Chapter 7, "Consequences for Common Concerns."

Meeting	Chapter Discussed	Activity	Homework
		their experiences; analyze and discuss.	2. Encourage parents to try out one or two consequences that relate to their problems.
11	Chapter 7	1. Discuss chapter. 2. Have parents share experiences; analyze and discuss.	1. Read Chapters 8 and 9, "Games Children Play" and "Approaches to Problems at School." 2. Try out one or two consequences.
12	Chapters 8 and 9	1. Discuss chapters. 2. Have parents share experiences; analyze and discuss.	1. Read Chapter 10, "The Family Meeting." 2. Try a family meeting. (Encourage taping.)
13	Chapter 10	1. Discuss chapter. 2. Have parents share tapes or discuss experiences; analyze and discuss.	Practice family meetings. (Encourage taping.)
14	Chapter 10	1. Have parents share tapes or discuss experiences; analyze and discuss.	1. Practice family meetings. 2. Read Chapter 11, "A Parent's Confidence-Building Guide to Effective Problem-Solving."

Meeting	Chapter Discussed	Activity	Homework
15	Chapters 10 and 11	1. Share tapes or experiences; analyze and discuss. 2. Discuss Chapter 11.	

General Guidelines for Discussions and Role Playing

When discussing a chapter, the leader is responsible for guiding the discussion. A good opening for a discussion might be "How did you feel about this chapter?" This usually begins an analysis of the material assigned. The leader can check the group's understanding of the material as the discussion progresses. Often the leader may need to ask for clarification with "Why do you feel that way?" If important points are not brought up, the leader can ask specific questions. As problems are discussed focus on the principles involved.

Role playing is a simple yet extremely helpful technique for demonstrating different approaches. The leader can play the role of the parent, while the parent plays his child. In this way he can provide a mirror for the parent or model an alternate way to respond. The leader can also ask other group members to role-play with the parent who shares the problem.

Each role-playing example should be evaluated by the players as well as the group. Suggested questions are: "How did you feel when I did that?" "What did the group notice happened when she said . . . ?" "When you said . . . , I felt . . ."

An Advanced Group

Once the book has been studied thoroughly as outlined, parents may wish to continue meeting together with a different meeting format. In the advanced group the meetings would be unstructured. In each meeting the participants would be responsible for bringing up problems for discussion. The dynamics of the behavior would be discussed and suggestions offered. References could be made to the book for review purposes based on individual need. Role playing could be utilized when appropriate.

REFERENCE

Ellis, Albert. *Reason and Emotion in Psychotherapy*. New York: Lyle Stuart, 1962.

Index